Wisdom for Teens

The Battle of Anxiety and Depression

Gary S. Park

Prayer

Dear God,

I pray for the reader who is facing unhappiness. I pray you will surround them with your love and peace and give them hope and strength to face their challenges. I pray that you will help them to see that they are not alone. Heal their hearts and minds, remove the darkness from their lives, and replace it with your light. Give them the courage to reach out for help when they need it. Allow their experiences to grow their faith and trust in you so that they will come to know your love and peace.

In Jesus' name, Amen.

Please know that you are not alone and that there are people who care about you and want to help. If you are struggling with depression, please reach out for help. Many resources are available to you, and you don't have to go through this alone.

Here are some resources that can help:

The National Suicide Prevention Lifeline: 1-800-273-8255

The Crisis Text Line: Text HOME to 741741

The Jed Foundation: https://www.jedfoundation.org/

The American Foundation for Suicide Prevention:

Contents

Introduction

In the dead of the night, 16-year-old Alex lay awake in his room, staring at the ceiling. The glow from the streetlight outside filtered through his window, casting long, ominous shadows on the walls. His mind was a whirlwind of thoughts, worries, and fears. An upcoming test, a friend he may have upset, a future he couldn't seem to visualize.

A heavy, invisible weight was pressing down on his chest, making it harder and harder to breathe. It was like drowning on dry land. He felt alone, like he was the only one going through this overwhelming battle. If you're a teenager reading this, you might recognize this scenario. If you're an adult, you might remember such moments from your own adolescence, or you've witnessed similar struggles in a teenager you cared about.

You may even feel similar burdens when thinking about a teenager in your own home. About one in three teenagers will experience anxiety. At any given time, around 20% of teenagers are battling depression. Six individuals fight unseen battles daily in a standard high school classroom of thirty students. It's no longer a rare occurrence or a phase we can shrug off; it's a pressing, prevalent issue that demands our attention, empathy, and action.

In our fast-paced world full of pressures and expectations, teenagers are grappling with anxiety and depression more than ever. As they navigate through the treacherous waters of adolescence, they must also confront these formidable adversaries that can make every day feel like a storm. But there is hope, and there is help. That's why this book exists.

Anxiety and depression are invisible enemies, and their impacts on your life can be devastating. When you're anxious, you may feel like your heart is constantly racing and your thoughts are spinning out of control. Even the simplest decisions can seem like insurmountable challenges. That upcoming exam, that party invitation, that text message that needs a response, all can trigger a storm of worries and fears.

You might feel like you're constantly on edge, waiting for the next big catastrophe to hit. You feel your palms sweat, your breath quickens, and it seems like the whole world is closing in on you. You're trying to keep up a brave front, pretending you're perfectly okay. Depression, on the other hand, feels like a deep, dark abyss. It's as if you're trapped in a never-ending tunnel with no light at the end.

You lose interest in things you once enjoyed. Every morning, it's a struggle to get out of bed. You feel exhausted all the time, yet sleep is elusive. Your appetite may be gone, or you might eat more than usual. You may feel a constant sense of worthlessness, guilt, and self-loathing. It's like wearing a mask you can't take off, forcing a smile when you only want to express yourself somehow, in some way.

It can feel isolating like you're alone in your struggles. You may feel misunderstood, judged, or stigmatized because of your anxiety or depression. It's challenging to articulate your feelings or even understand them yourself. You might feel like you're a burden to others, or they wouldn't understand. And perhaps the most unbearable is the guilt and frustration you might feel for not being able to 'snap out of it' despite your best efforts. You're not alone in feeling this way.

But it's not just about you, the teenager. Parents, teachers, and others who interact with teenagers also struggle. You might be grappling with helplessness, confusion, or guilt, unsure of how to help or what to say. You want to support them, but it's hard to understand what they're going through if you've never experienced it.

In reading "Wisdom for Teens: The Battle of Anxiety and Depression," you'll find a treasure trove of understanding, comfort, and practical guidance. One of the most significant benefits you'll gain is a deeper comprehension of what anxiety and depression really are. This book will offer insights into the science behind these mental health challenges, detailing how they affect your brain and body, helping to debunk myths, and removing the shroud of stigma that often surrounds these issues.

This book will also provide valuable tools to help you manage your anxiety and depression. You'll discover effective coping strategies, relaxation techniques, and mindfulness exercises specifically tailored to the teenage experience. We'll explore how to handle panic attacks, quiet a racing mind, lift your mood, and regain control when you're feeling overwhelmed.

Each chapter will feature real-life examples and interactive conditioning, making applying the lessons to your own experiences easier. This book is designed to empower you. It will provide you with the knowledge and tools to actively manage your mental health. By understanding your triggers, you'll learn to anticipate and mitigate bouts of anxiety or depressive episodes.

This proactive approach can lead to greater confidence and a sense of control over your life, which can significantly improve your mental well-being. If you're a parent, teacher, or counselor reading this book, it will enhance your understanding of what teenagers with anxiety and depression go through. This empathy will better equip you to offer them the support they need.

You'll also find guidance on initiating and maintaining open conversations about mental health and encouraging teenagers to seek professional help when needed. Most importantly, this book will remind you that you are not alone. Each page will resonate with the experiences of countless others who are on a similar journey. It will inspire hope, resilience, and self-empowerment, showing you that there is a path to a healthier, happier you even amidst the challenges.

This book isn't just a guide; it's a friend, an ally in your battle against anxiety and depression. I've walked the same path you're walking now. I stared at the ceiling at night, besieged by anxious thoughts that wouldn't cease. I've grappled with the heavy, relentless pull of depression. As a teenager, I faced my own battles, which felt lonely and overwhelming at times.

I also wondered if anyone else could understand the hurricane of emotions and worries that were my constant companions. When I say I know what it feels like to be consumed by worry, to feel as though happiness is an elusive dream, I'm speaking from personal experience. It was a difficult journey, a winding path filled with obstacles and setbacks, but I learned, grew, and found my way. There were many days when I was the hero, and other times I watched the world pass.

Over the years, I've poured myself into understanding anxiety and depression, not just the clinical definitions and medical treatments but the raw, real-life experiences. I've spoken to countless teenagers who, like me, struggled with these invisible enemies. I've listened to their stories, shared their trials and triumphs, and learned from them.

As I battled my issues and separations, I started documenting my experiences, the techniques that worked for me, and those that didn't. I also noted the insights I gained from the wisdom shared by others and the lessons learned from my studies. This book culminates all those experiences, insights, and knowledge woven together to provide practical guidance and compassionate understanding.

Why am I the right person to guide you? Because I've been there. I've fought the battles you're fighting. I've been emotionally hurt before. I've said some things I've regretted for years, wishing I could take back years later. My school was no different than yours, filled with dysfunction, anger, frustration, bullying, heartbreaks, abuse, drugs, mean girls, terrible guys, suicides, car accidents, bad teachers, a failed system, and everyone trying to do their best to get through. We had great teachers and parents who cared, but the burden for some juveniles was overwhelming.

Some teens didn't have either parent, or one of their parents visited once a week! Others had a new parent who stepped up to the plate and took a swing at parenting someone else's kids. Many young adults are so focused on developing outside relationships that they forget about their schoolwork, end up in summer school, or get held back. A few of these teens said, "Screw it, I quit!" and then dropped out of high school. Half of those came back for their GED later on.

How many of us know someone killed by a DUI driver? My brother lost the love of his life, and it took 15 years to calm down his heartache. I've lost friends, coworkers, and family members to suicide and accidental suicide. And there's a great chance your parents and their parents have seen, heard, and lived it just like many of us do each day.

Everything is serious, and it affects adults forever. Teens push things down deep inside, the same way an adult does. The difference is that an adult has pressed so much down over the years that it doesn't take too much to get emotional about it. They understand and feel it; I promise they have hidden stories they've tried to forget and overcome.

Here's a secret: The truth is you can never overcome the burdens of life. You have a heart, mind, and soul that will grasp these emotions and hold them dear. What you can do is learn to rise above; that doesn't mean forgetting, just simply elevating your mindset with knowledge and wisdom. And with God's help, all things are possible!

I've learned how to manage my mental health and live a fulfilling life despite the challenges, and I want to help you do the same. This book is more than just pages filled with information; it's a testament to resilience, a beacon of hope, and tangible proof that you can overcome anything. I offer knowledge, empathy, and understanding because I've lived and grown from it.

And to be honest, I don't want anyone to suffer from these issues. I want to help as many people as possible to reduce and diminish these burdens.

It's time to take control of your life, to break free from the shackles of uncertainty and fear. It's time to empower yourself with the knowledge to help you navigate life's challenges confidently and gracefully. Don't let the obstacles of the past hold you back; instead, arm yourself with the coping strategies that will help you overcome them.

Find the resilience within you, tap into your inner strength, and begin your journey toward a stronger, healthier, and happier you. The right book, the right guide, and the right time are all here, waiting for you to embrace them. Don't wait any longer; seize the opportunity to transform your life.

You deserve to live a life full of joy, purpose, and fulfillment. Don't let anything hold you back from achieving your dreams. The power to change your life is within your grasp; all you need to do is embrace it. So go ahead, take that first step, and start living the life that you were meant to live.

Chapter One

The Reality of Depression

Teenagers facing depression encounter more than just a brief period of feeling down or a few days of being in an isolated mood. Depression is a cognitive health condition that can impact their daily life, interactions, and performance at school or work. Adolescence is a time of significant change and stress, making depression even more difficult to manage. This first chapter goes into the intricacies of teenage depression, providing insight into its nature, how it varies from depression in younger children, and the typical signs to watch for.

Depression, often termed major depressive disorder or clinical depression, can be a significant mental health condition that impacts individuals of all ages, from children to adults. Its reach extends to every aspect of a teenager's life: school, relationships, physical health, and overall sense of self.

Everything goes beyond experiencing sadness or facing a difficult time. It demands comprehension, care, and an effective recuperation strategy. By identifying the symptoms early, receiving a diagnosis, and pursuing a treatment plan that could encompass medication, psychotherapy, healthy lifestyle choices, and a reliable support system, numerous adolescents can triumph over depression.

Adolescence is a period of influential, physical, emotional, and psychological changes, including changes in the brain. It's a crucial stage where teenagers develop their identity, gain independence, and grapple with new social roles. Simultaneously, the teenage brain is still maturing, particularly the area responsible for impulse control and decision-making, known as the prefrontal cortex.

This convergence of developmental changes and brain development can lead to emotional disruption, making teenagers particularly prone to depression. Add external stressors like academic pressures and social difficulties, not to mention family problems, to the mix, and it's easy to understand why many teenagers struggle with depression.

As we learn more about depression, it becomes clear that how it affects and influences people can vary depending on their age. Depression in children is not the same as in teenagers, and it's essential to recognize these differences to provide the most effective treatment. Childhood depression can be challenging to identify.

Depressed Children vs. Teenagers

Unlike teenagers or adults, young children may not have the vocabulary to express their feelings, making it challenging for parents and caregivers to recognize the signs. Some of the common symptoms of depression in children include:

- Persistent sadness or unhappiness

- Decreased interest in activities they used to enjoy

- Frequent crying

- Increased irritability or anger

- Difficulty concentrating

- Physical headaches or stomachaches

- Changes in appetite or sleep

- Poor performance in school or social interactions

Children's depressive feelings might be related to family conflict or fear of academic failure, boredom, isolation from being smaller, and not being able to participate with others.

Depression in Teenagers

When it comes to teenagers, depression can often look quite different. Teenagers are more capable of articulating their feelings, but they may not always choose to do so. Depression can manifest in many ways; one common symptom is a lack of motivation. Teens may find it difficult to concentrate or feel motivated to do anything. Emotions may flow, feeling that you don't deserve happiness. Another common symptom is losing interest in activities they used to enjoy. Sports, hobbies, or spending time with friends may no longer hold the same appeal that they once did.

This withdrawal from friends and family can be difficult to witness, as the individual may avoid going out or socializing altogether. This leads to loneliness and isolation for everyone. The teen may have difficulty concentrating or remembering things and need help making decisions or following through on tasks. Restlessness and agitation can also be present, leading the individual to fidget or pace and have trouble sitting still.

Changes in sleep patterns are another concern; later on, fatigue and a lack of energy set in. The individual may feel insecure about their body image, struggle with acne, or face challenges related to their sexual development.

Teenagers may experience changes in their mood, such as being irritable, angry, or anxious. They may also have trouble controlling their emotions. They might experience changes in their behavior, leading to activities they usually wouldn't do, such as getting a little destructive, skipping school, or getting into trouble. At the same time, teenagers might experience depression in response to interpersonal relationships and significant life changes, such as parents getting divorced or moving to a new area.

When experiencing new encounters, it leads to emotional confusion. This confusion often manifests in various behavioral changes, such as becoming more withdrawn or even demonstrating more tantrums or acting out. This is why parents and guardians need to be aware of the signs and symptoms of depression in children and teenagers.

Teenagers are in a transitional stage. They are shifting from childhood to adulthood, navigating complex emotional landscapes, and grappling with self-identity and autonomy. Their cognitive abilities allow them to understand their depressive feelings better. Still, societal pressures, the struggle for acceptance, and the fear of stigma may lead them to hide their feelings or avoid seeking help.

Addressing Depression: Children vs. Teens

Given these differences, the approaches to help anyone with depression must be tailored accordingly. It's important to note that parents, teachers, and caregivers play a crucial role in detecting signs of depression in children. Since children might struggle to express their feelings, it's up to adults to be observant of any behavioral changes.

Early intervention often involves a combination of family therapy by managing problems and changing how each thinks and behaves. Treatment and medication are often the go-to solutions for teenagers, but it's important to take a holistic approach considering the individual's social and family circumstances. Ultimately, the most effective treatment plan is one that is personalized to the unique needs of each person. Address the issue; don't flock toward medication.

While parental and adult support remains crucial for teenagers, strategies to address depression might also involve peer support groups, individual therapy, and school-based mental health programs. Encouraging open conversations about mental health, teaching coping strategies, and fostering resilience can be beneficial in managing mixed feelings and emotions.

Understanding the specific needs and experiences of teenagers allows us to address depression in a way that respects their individual experiences and provides the most effective support. It's not just about acknowledging the presence of depression but about adapting our approach to their unique needs and ensuring they don't feel alone in their struggle.

When tackling the problem of teens, it's essential to understand the significance of establishing a secure and encouraging setting in which they can freely express their emotions and share their encounters. Establishing such an environment can be facilitated by parents, teachers, and caregivers. Ensure you're not leading the witness, and allow them to explain their emotions. The gathered information can be used to raise awareness of what's happening at school, within the neighborhood, and on the internet to help isolate what's causing childhood and teenage depression.

Chapter Two

Impacts of Negativity

Negativity, that gloomy cloud that often descends without warning, is something we all experience at some point in our lives. But for teenagers, it can be particularly intense and overwhelming, especially from multiple directions such as home, school, or even the war within themselves. This chapter looks closely at the negative effects of this bad energy. It shows how it slips into our thoughts, feelings, and actions and makes the battles with anxiety and depression even tougher.

It will dissect the sources of negativity, starting with life and family situations and then moving on to the pressures of school and academics. Finally, it will highlight the corrosive effects of how negativity feeds depression. As we journey through these topics, remember that understanding these issues is the first crucial step in developing strategies to tackle and overcome them. Stay resilient, and know that you're not alone in this battle.

Negativity can sneak into our lives in many ways, but one of the most influential and often underappreciated sources is our family and home environment. Family isn't just about the genetic ties that bind us together. It's the first social circle we encounter, our first taste of relationship dynamics, and the initial arena where we learn to navigate emotions and conflicts. As such, negativity in this sphere can leave a lasting impression on us, especially as teenagers.

You see, families, like any other social unit, can be as diverse as the rainbow. Some families provide a nurturing, positive environment that encourages personal growth and emotional well-being. Others, unfortunately, can be the main cause of negative feelings, marked by constant arguing, harsh criticism, or, in some cases, emotional neglect. For teenagers who are in the critical stage of forming their identities and worldviews, such negative environments can amplify feelings of anxiety and depression.

Perhaps you've had to deal with constant criticism from a parent who seems never satisfied with your achievements, or you're caught in the crossfire of endless parental conflicts. And possibly, those issues have turned into a divorce and living in a separated family.

Divorce isn't easy for anyone, not even for the parents. Children shouldn't have to suffer because of two adults who can't get along. Life isn't fair, and when there's an imbalance in your own home, feelings of anger, confusion, and frustration start stacking up. Some children don't see one of their parents anymore. While some families are in a 50/50 relationship, moving to one parent's house for a week and then back to the other throughout the year.

Maybe you feel ignored or unloved in your own home, as if you're living under the same roof with strangers. Whatever the case may be, it's important to understand that such experiences can have a deep impact on your emotional well-being. On the flip side, you can grow without those family arguments while feeling strong and solidified. A broken family isn't caused by a divorce; it's a household of conflict where everything is counterproductive. Parents who choose to separate can begin their own healing adventure by turning a brokenness into a healthier life.

Most teens faced with family separation find themselves replacing one of those parents, doing more chores, and taking an active role in their respective households. In doing so, they find themselves growing up too early, and many never get to live their life. This is not to say that all family conflict or criticism is inherently negative or damaging. After all, disagreements are a normal part of life, and constructive criticism can foster personal growth.

The problem arises when these instances become the norm rather than the exception once they carry a level of intensity that leaves you feeling sad, worthless, or constantly on edge. Naturally, there are no easy approaches for families as each one takes one day at a time, hoping each week is better than the last. There's nothing better than having a balanced life with two loving parents. But in the event you're missing one of them, God will always be there as your guide.

Your family's negative situation does not define you. You are not responsible for your family's problems, and you cannot control their behavior. However, you can control how you react to their behavior. You can choose to focus on the positive aspects of your life, and you can choose to build relationships with people who support you.

You are not alone in this experience. Many people come from families with negative situations. There are church support groups and online forums where you can connect with others who understand what you're going through. You are not alone, and there is help available. There's a whole world out there beyond the confines of your current home environment.

When you're ready, you can start exploring the world outside of your home. You can meet new people, learn new things, and experience new adventures. You can find support and love from friends, community members, or your part-time job. There are always people who will lend a helping hand.

Reach out to your friends and other family members and let them know what you are going through. You can also find support from community organizations, such as churches, schools, and youth centers. Even your friend's parents can be a valuable source of support. If you're feeling lost or alone, talk to someone you trust. I can't count how much wisdom and knowledge I've obtained from my friend's parents.

It's amazing how much others can offer us, especially during challenging times. Sometimes, it can be difficult to talk to our own family as we may feel judged or that they're too close to the situation. However, speaking with other adults can be incredibly helpful as they're often the best listeners. By tapping into their wealth of experience and knowledge, we can benefit greatly by allowing them to share their backgrounds with us.

When you're feeling happy or alone, you can always turn to God for comfort and guidance. God is always there for you, no matter what. You can communicate all of your thoughts, and He will listen. God can give you comfort in your pain and guide you through your challenges. Maybe you're feeling emptiness in your heart, and you don't want to live depressed. You hold the gift of having God in your life. He will give you purpose and ease your suffering. This has nothing to do with religion; Jesus didn't come to save the world from their sins and suffering by preaching a religion. He wants a relationship with you to strengthen your faith. He will guide and protect you, leading you to a heavenly home after this life is the ultimate goal.

Schoolwork Concerns and Depression

School is a significant part of a teenager's life. It's the place where you learn and grow, make friends, and start figuring out your place in the world. However, school can also be a source of intense pressure and stress. The demands of schoolwork, the expectations of teachers and parents, and the pressure to fit in socially can build up, often leading to feelings of anxiety and depression.

Academic pressure is a common factor. You might be trying to juggle multiple assignments, prepare for exams, or keep up with demanding coursework. Perhaps you're worried about your future, getting into a good college, choosing the right career path, or meeting your parent's high expectations. This constant feeling of being under pressure can be overwhelming and exhausting, leading to feelings of helplessness and hopelessness, hallmarks of depression.

Teenagers are naturally social creatures, and they want to be accepted by their peers. However, the pressure to fit in can be overwhelming, and it leads to making unhealthy choices. For example, you may try to change your appearance, personality, or interests in order to fit in. You may also engage in risky behaviors, such as drug use or drinking, to be accepted by your peers.

Perhaps you're feeling left out and can quickly feel emotional or rejected. This can be especially true if someone feels different than their peers, such as their race, ethnicity, religion, or sexual orientation. Feeling left out can lead to loneliness, isolation, and sadness. It can also make teenagers more vulnerable to bullying and other forms of social harassment.

Bullying is a severe problem that can have a devastating impact on teenagers. Bullies can make teenagers feel worthless, insecure, and afraid. They can also lead to emotional and physical harm. If you're being bullied, it's essential to tell a trusted adult, such as a parent, teacher, or school principal. You don't have to handle anything alone; there are people to help you. Don't ever keep it to yourself; the problem will never go away until you bring the issue to someone's attention.

Teenagers may feel the need to conform to the expectations of their peers. This can lead to them making choices they're not comfortable with, such as dressing a certain way or listening to certain music. Conforming can lead to teenagers suppressing their true selves and their individuality. We aren't a herd of cattle chasing after one ideology; you're unique and can be yourself.

Teenage friendships and relationships can be complex and challenging. Teenagers are still learning how to navigate these relationships, and they'll make mistakes. They may also be hurt or disappointed by their friends or partners. The fear of judgment or exclusion from friends or partners can be a heavy emotional burden.

It's alright if you want to have someone close; you're still developing emotionally and mentally and may not be ready for the emotional demands of a serious relationship. You might be more likely to make impulsive decisions or act without thinking about the consequences.

Teenagers of all ages work at communicating their feelings and may not know how to resolve conflicts in a healthy way. This leads to misunderstandings, disputes, and even break-ups. You may feel pressure from friends to date certain people or to behave in specific ways in those relationships. This can make it difficult for each one to make their own choices and to follow their own hearts. The youths of today can be very jealous, leading to problems in any relationship. If the teen is dating, they may be worried that their partner will cheat on them or that they will be replaced by someone else. This jealousy can manifest in controlling behavior, possessiveness, or even violence.

Teenagers may have unrealistic expectations about what a relationship should be like. They may not realize that all relationships have ups and downs. Each may be influenced by unrealistic portrayals of relationships. Movies and TV shows often depict relationships as being perfect and without conflict. This can give teenagers unrealistic expectations about what a relationship should be like.

Young men and women are at different stages of life than adults, which can sometimes lead to problems in their relationships. As adults have more life experience, they have different expectations from a relationship than what a teenager could comprehend. This can lead to conflict and misunderstandings, especially if teens believe they know more than adults.

And since you're going through a lot of changes, both physically and emotionally. You'll try to figure out who you are and what you can become. High school relationships can be a big part of this journey. For many teenagers, their high school relationship is the most significant thing in the world without realizing there is life after high school.

There are a few reasons why teenagers don't see the big picture. First, high school is when teenagers spend a lot of time with their friends and classmates. They are often surrounded by other couples, and it can seem like everyone is in a relationship. This can make teenagers feel like they need to be in a relationship to fit in.

Second, teenagers are going through a lot of emotional changes. They are dealing with hormones, potential peer pressure, and the stress of school itself. A high school relationship can provide a sense of stability and support during this time. It can also give teenagers a feeling of being loved and accepted other than the affection from home.

Third, teenagers are still learning about themselves and what they want in a relationship. A high school relationship can be a great way to experiment and learn what works for them. It can also help them to develop their communication and conflict-resolution skills.

Of course, not all high school relationships are successful. Most relationships end in heartbreak and disappointment. However, even these experiences can be valuable learning opportunities for teenagers. They can learn how to deal with rejection, how to move on from a relationship, and how to be a better partner in the future.

Overall, high school relationships can be a positive experience for teenagers. They can provide love, support, and a sense of belonging. It's important for teenagers to remember that high school relationships are not the most important thing in the world. There is so much more to life than dating, and teenagers should focus on their education, personal goals, their friends, and their family.

Moreover, the virtual world and the use of technology in education can add another layer of stress for teenagers. The pressure to be always connected, always available, and always responsive can be exhausting. Teenagers are constantly bombarded with messages and notifications, and they may feel like they need to be constantly online in order to keep up.

Cyberbullying can be very difficult to escape. Bullies can reach their victims 24/7, and it can be hard to find a safe place to escape harassment. It can be very public. Bullies can post embarrassing or hurtful messages online, where they can be seen by a large audience. This can make victims feel humiliated and ashamed.

They can have a lasting impact. Victims of cyberbullying may have trouble sleeping, eating, and concentrating. They may also withdraw from friends and family. In some cases, cyberbullying can lead to depression, anxiety, and even suicide. It can be very damaging to teenagers, who are already vulnerable to peer pressure and criticism.

The pressure to be constantly connected can be overwhelming for teenagers. They may feel like they must frequently check their phones and social accounts, even when they're supposed to study or spend time with their families. This can lead to extra anxiety and stress, leading to feelings of fear, isolation, and worthlessness.

In recognizing these challenges, it's crucial to remember that it's okay to feel overwhelmed. It's okay to feel like everything is too much. School is a challenging environment, and it's completely normal to feel stressed out. But what's important is how you respond to these challenges and pressures and manage your mental health in the face of these stressors.

Not to push any buttons out there, but some adults still have issues from their high school days that keep repeating over again because "someone" didn't move on with their lives. It's not uncommon for adults to still have issues from their high school years that keep repeating themselves. This can happen for several reasons. Some adults may have experienced trauma during their youth, such as bullying, abuse, neglect, and two handfuls of bad moments.

This trauma can have an everlasting impact on their mental health and can lead to problems in their adult life. Grown-ups may have developed unhealthy coping mechanisms to deal with the stress of high school. These coping mechanisms, such as substance abuse or self-harm, can continue into adulthood and can make it difficult to move on.

Adults may participate in negative self-talk that developed during their high school years. These harmful internal discussions and intrusive thoughts can keep them stuck in the past and prevent them from moving on with their lives. Some adults may have a fear of failure that developed during their high school years. This fear of failure can control their minds and keep them from taking risks and trying new things in adulthood.

Chapter Three

How Negativity Feeds Depression

I n the whirlwind of teenage life, it's easy to get caught up in the wave of negativity, not realizing the extent to which it can compound the challenges of depression. So, let's take a moment to understand how negative thoughts can make depression worse. Knowing this, we can start to find ways to free ourselves from its grip.

One key concept to grasp is that our minds have a tendency to focus on negative experiences and give them more weight than positive ones. This is known as the negativity bias, and it's a survival mechanism that has been passed down to us from our predecessors. However, this bias can become overwhelming and lead to feelings of depression when we focus too much on failures and criticisms instead of successes and praise.

It's crucial to recognize this tendency and try to balance it out with positive experiences and perspectives. By doing so, we can avoid letting our negative thoughts and emotions take over and maintain a healthy outlook on life. Consider how this might play out in your own life. You may have received mostly positive feedback on a project, but you can't stop thinking about the one criticism. Or perhaps you had a great day at school, but your mood plummeted over a minor argument with a friend. Recognizing the presence of a negativity bias is an important step in challenging it.

Negativity can create a vicious cycle, especially when it's tied to depression. It often starts with a single negative thought or event. This negativity colors your emotions, which in turn affects your actions, potentially leading to more negative experiences. The cycle then repeats, amplifying the negativity each time around.

Have you ever experienced a negative thought spiral? For instance, have you ever convinced yourself that you're going to fail an upcoming test? It's easy to feel down and discouraged. Unfortunately, this type of thinking can actually hold you back from taking action and studying for the test. This can then lead to poor performance on the test, which only validates your negative beliefs and strengthens the cycle. Negative self-talk is the inner voice that perpetuates feelings of inadequacy and worthlessness symptoms of depression. Remember, it's important to challenge negative thoughts and focus on positive actions to break the cycle to achieve success.

Have you ever caught yourself making negative statements about yourself? Maybe you've said things like "I'm not good enough," "I can't do this," or "Nobody likes me." These kinds of statements can slowly eat away at your confidence, making it harder to feel good and move forward. Being aware of your core identity is integral to forming healthy attachments within anything you're trying to accomplish.

Not being aware of your shortcomings and strengths means you will find it extremely difficult to regain your self-esteem and keep moving forward. You must care for your physical and mental well-being before these negative thoughts start owning you.

Self-awareness can be highly beneficial for mental health. The first person to benefit from becoming more self-aware is you. You can learn to become more proactive by developing into the best version of yourself.

Your confidence, decisions, and communication skills can become sharper. You can learn to be more compassionate to yourself and can see things from other people's perspectives.

Prioritizing your thoughts and actions in front of others will help you take control of your own happiness and well-being. As the famous saying goes, "You owe it to yourself to be happy." You can adopt a positive outlook, let go of minor issues, and not take things too personally. Understanding how your negativity feeds into depression will be the focus point in getting any better. This comprehension will pave the way for practical strategies to disrupt the cycle of negative thinking. You want to challenge the negativity and replace it with more positive, supportive internal dialogue. When you put in the time and effort to study hard and achieve your goals, it can actually reduce your stress levels.

By focusing on your academic or professional pursuits, you're taking control of your future and working toward a better life for yourself. This can give you a sense of purpose and fulfillment, which can help to alleviate feelings of stress and anxiety. So, the next time you feel overwhelmed, remember that investing in yourself and your education can be a powerful antidote to stress.

Taking one step at a time or focusing on one obstacle can be incredibly important when it comes to building confidence. By breaking down a larger goal into smaller, more manageable pieces, you can avoid feeling overwhelmed and stay motivated as you work toward your objective. Each small success can help to build momentum and boost your confidence, making it easier to tackle the next challenge. You'll be amazed at what you can achieve.

Loss of Time, Losing Focus

The explosion of new digital communication has profoundly transformed our lives. These platforms have brought countless benefits. They are connecting us with friends and family across the globe, giving us access to infinite knowledge, and providing platforms to express ourselves. But alongside these benefits, social media can also breed and amplify negativity, which can escalate feelings of depression.

Everybody is beginning to take notice that the internet is a major distraction. With so many notifications, messages, and updates constantly bombarding our screens, it can be difficult to stay focused on our goals. Whether it's checking your status every few minutes or scrolling through feeds for hours on end, videos and social influencers can quickly consume our time and attention.

This can be especially problematic when we're trying to accomplish something important, such as studying for an exam or completing a school project. Instead of letting social media take over our lives, we need to be mindful of how we use it and set clear boundaries for ourselves. By limiting our time with electronics and prioritizing our goals, we can stay on track and achieve the success we desire. Remember, every small step counts, so stay focused.

How to stay focused

When it comes to accomplishing important tasks, eliminate any distractions that may hinder our progress. Some of the biggest culprits of distraction in today's society are video games, telephone calls, television shows, and trying to find out what everyone's doing. With constant notifications and updates, it can be difficult to resist the urge to check our phones and scroll through our feeds. However, if we truly want to achieve success, we must learn to turn off these distractions.

Anything that pulls you away from what you're supposed to be doing is a distraction. You'll be more prepared each and every day by ensuring you've done your best to prepare for anything heading your way or currently in front of you. By doing so, we can stay focused and motivated to accomplish our short and long-term goals. Remember, the key to success is discipline and determination. So, let's stop those distractions and stay on track toward achieving our dreams.

When we have free time, we often curate our lives on the internet to present an ideal image, a highlight reel that doesn't reflect the complexity and challenges of everyday life. As a result, when you scroll through your feeds and see your peers achieving, smiling, and seemingly living perfect lives, it's easy to feel inadequate or believe you're not measuring up. This phenomenon, known as social comparison, can feed negativity and contribute to feelings of depression.

It's also worth noting that excessive use of cyberspace leads to virtual isolation. People online compare themselves to others and feel pressure to constantly keep up with their online presence. When you encounter issues, posted statements, or photos, it can drive your emotions, feeding negativity when you least expect it.

It's important to balance our digital lives with real-life interactions to maintain a healthy and fulfilling social life. Many people still prefer physical books over digital ones. There's something about holding a book in your hands, feeling the pages turn, and smelling the paper that can't be replicated with a digital device. Plus, reading a book can help reduce screen time and give your eyes a break.

In today's digital age, it's easy to spend hours scrolling through video feeds, news articles, and other online content. This can often leave us feeling drained, anxious, or overwhelmed. Take a break from screen time and negativity by picking up a fiction book. It can transport you to a different world and provide an escape from reality for a while. Alternatively, if you're looking for a more hands-on approach to relaxation, consider trying out a Sudoku or maze book.

These fun and challenging puzzle games can provide a great mental workout and help you unwind while giving your brain the stimulation it needs. So why not give yourself a chance to recharge and refocus by taking a break from the digital world and engaging in some good old-fashioned puzzle-solving?

Chapter Four

Unhealthy Coping Mechanisms

The struggle with depression often extends beyond the feelings of sadness and despair themselves. It encompasses a range of behaviors and habits that emerge as coping mechanisms. While some coping strategies can be beneficial, others can exacerbate the problem, leading to a vicious cycle of worsening symptoms. In this chapter, we'll explore some of the unhealthy coping mechanisms that teenagers often resort to when dealing with depression.

Understanding these patterns is crucial not just for teenagers themselves but also for parents, educators, and mental health professionals working to support them. Depression can prompt a variety of responses, some of which are counterproductive and even harmful. Apathy, the cycle of self-doubt, and smartphone addiction are among the common unhealthy coping mechanisms we often see in depressed teenagers.

Apathy and Fleeing

Apathy is characterized by indifference or a lack of interest, concern, or enthusiasm. It's a state of numbness where individuals detach themselves emotionally from their surroundings. When faced with depression, some teenagers might respond with apathy to protect themselves from pain or disappointment. Apathy might manifest as neglecting schoolwork, lacking interest in social activities, or not caring about personal hobbies and passions.

Teens may have lost their spark or motivation. The danger of apathy is that it can exacerbate feelings of isolation and worthlessness, intensifying the depressive state. Emotionally, teens might disconnect from their senses, refusing to acknowledge or discuss them. Physically, they might isolate themselves from family and friends, spend more time alone in their rooms, or lose interest in social activities.

Fleeing is a problematic coping mechanism as it often unaddressed the underlying issues, allowing depression to take an even firmer hold. Additionally, it can lead to increased loneliness, feelings of guilt, and a sense of hopelessness. While apathy and fleeing might initially serve as protective mechanisms, allowing teens to distance themselves from emotional pain, they can feed into the depressive cycle, worsening feelings of loneliness and disconnection.

Recognizing these unhealthy coping mechanisms is crucial to understanding the complexity of teenage depression and working toward healthier coping strategies. When teens respond to depression with apathy, they create an emotional void. This indifference may temporarily numb the pain but also strips away joy, excitement, and motivation. It may lead to a lack of fulfillment in life and reinforce feelings of emptiness and worthlessness, strengthening the grip of depression.

Similarly, fleeing may provide temporary relief from distressing situations or feelings. However, it fails to address the common denominator of depression. Avoidance does not lead to resolution. The unaddressed issues and unprocessed emotions continue to linger, potentially deepening the depressive state.

The good news is that these unhealthy coping mechanisms can be unlearned and replaced with healthier alternatives. But the first step toward this is recognition and understanding. Understanding these mechanisms is crucial for parents, teachers, and mental health professionals to provide the proper support. It allows for a more empathetic approach, recognizing that these responses are not mere acts of rebellion or laziness but cries for help.

Moving forward, it's essential to open communication channels, offer support, and encourage healthier coping mechanisms such as setting small achievable goals, practicing mindfulness or meditation, engaging in physical exercise, pursuing hobbies or interests, seeking social support, and maintaining a healthy diet and sleep routine. Remember that this process takes time, patience, and a lot of understanding. Be patient with yourself or the teenager you're supporting, and remember that each step forward, no matter how small, is a victory.

The Cycle of Self-doubt and Depression

The experience of depression often intertwines with feelings of self-doubt, creating a cycle that can be challenging to break. Understanding this cycle is a vital step toward empowering anyone navigating their way out of it. Self-doubt can emerge from various sources. For some, it might be the result of continuous negative self-talk. For others, it could stem from criticism, negative feedback, or comparison with peers.

Regardless of its origin, self-doubt can become a formidable obstacle, eroding self-confidence and amplifying feelings of worthlessness, both common symptoms of depression. In a teenager's world, self-doubt may manifest in different areas: academic performance, physical appearance, social status, or abilities. It can affect decision-making, deter the pursuit of interests, and inhibit the willingness to explore new opportunities. When a teenager is also plagued by self-doubt, a damaging cycle can take root. The depressive state can fuel self-doubt, which, in turn, can intensify feelings of despair and hopelessness.

Teens may avoid situations challenging their decisions, leading to missed opportunities and worsening depression. To break this cycle, surrounding yourself with positive and supportive people can also help you stay motivated and confident in your decisions. Remember, it's okay to have doubts, but it's important not to let them control your life.

Positive self-talk fosters self-confidence, resilience, and emotional well-being. Teens can cultivate positive self-talk by monitoring and challenging negative thoughts, like replacing "I'm terrible at math" with "I'm working hard to improve my math skills." You'll be proactive by finding areas where you're weak and obtaining knowledge in those areas to redefine how you think.

You can become more positive and empowered by challenging negative thoughts and building resilience. Resilience is key to breaking the cycle of negativity and learning to navigate setbacks. Teens can develop resilience by maintaining a supportive social network, learning stress management techniques, setting realistic goals, and having a growth mindset. Recognizing and addressing patterns of self-doubt can help break the cycle of depression. Understanding the relationship between self-doubt and depression can help teenagers regain control over their thoughts, feelings, and lives.

Traditionally, schoolwork is only one of the issues at hand. It's most likely how they feel around other teens, from how they look, dress, and, honestly, how they communicate with others. Young women might judge one another based on looks and appearances and can be darn right evil, giving each other comments or causing gossip behind people's backs. As for young men, it could be a coolness factor combining attitude, visual impressions, and communication abilities as a few examples. Both parties are trying to discover who they are, what they can accomplish, and whether or not they follow what the crowd is doing.

So many teens are looking for elbow room during their life adventures, searching for the correct boundary lines of who they are and who they desire to become. During these avenues, each person needs to learn how to express themselves in a healthy way while trying to avoid the negativity of school and personal life. From socializing to developing friendships and engaging in the dating scene, communication is integral to our lives. Though the world expects us to have adequate communication skills, it cannot be taught and must be learned through personal experience.

Depression Released by Friendships

It may be easy to maintain surface-level relationships with acquaintances. However, building deep and meaningful connections requires intentional communication and time. In friendships, building trust, understanding, and mutual support can help alleviate depression by shifting the focus from a solo mindset to a team mentality. By being intentional, you want to be available and listen; when people see you care, they will care about you.

When you show genuine concern for someone's well-being, they'll likely remember you in a positive light, which can lead to mutual goodwill between the two of you. It's like the saying, "What you give, you get back." Or "What goes around comes around." Great friendships are built on a foundation of open and honest communication, where both parties feel comfortable sharing their thoughts, feelings, and experiences. This type of communication requires active listening, empathy, and a willingness to be vulnerable.

When communicating with friends, actively listening and giving them your full attention is essential. This means putting aside distractions like phones or other tasks and focusing on what they say. Additionally, empathy is crucial to building solid friendships. Putting yourself in your friend's shoes and trying to understand their perspective can create a deeper connection and show that you care about their feelings. If you have one best friend, it'll make your world a better place.

Vulnerability is a critical component of solid friendships. Sharing your feelings, thoughts, and experiences can create a safe space for your friend to do the same. This type of vulnerability requires trust and a willingness to be open and honest with one another. In the context of the dating scene, communication is equally important. While playing games or holding back your feelings may be tempting, being honest and direct is the best way to build a healthy relationship. This requires communication skills like active listening, empathy, and assertiveness.

No matter who you are, don't put everything out there. While being open and vulnerable in close relationships is essential, it's also important to exercise caution regarding acquaintances. Sharing too much personal information or emotions with people who haven't earned your trust can leave you vulnerable to manipulation or exploitation.

Not everyone has your best interests at heart. Some people may use personal information or vulnerabilities against you, either intentionally or unintentionally. That's why it's important to be discerning about who you share personal information with and to set boundaries around what you're comfortable sharing. When interacting with acquaintances, it's okay to keep some information private. You don't have to share everything about your life or emotions if you don't feel comfortable doing so.

Instead, focus on building mutual respect and producing trust over time. As you get to know someone better and develop a stronger relationship, you can choose to share more personal information if you feel up to it. Ultimately, it's up to you to decide how much information you want to share. By being discerning and setting those boundaries, you can protect yourself while still building meaningful connections with others.

If issues are already in action, be the better person and rise above versus adding fuel to the fire. You will always mold yourself by how you handle stress, anger, frustrations, and outbursts.

Outside Validation

Many factors can factor into depression, including genetics, environmental factors, and life experiences. One factor that may not immediately come to mind but can significantly impact mental health is the comments of parents. Parents are often the first people in a child's life that they look to for guidance, support, and validation. When parents comment negatively or criticize their children, it can damage their self-esteem and sense of self-worth. This can lead to feelings of hopelessness, worthlessness, and despair, which are all common symptoms of depression.

When parents comment negatively about or to their child, it can lead to the child internalizing these messages and believing that they are true. This can lead to a pattern of negative self-talk, where the child constantly puts themselves down and criticizes their actions and abilities. Over time, this negative self-talk can become deeply ingrained and difficult to overcome.

Another way that parent comments can lead to depression is through the development of learned helplessness. When parents are overly critical or harsh towards their child, it can make the child feel like they can never do anything right. This leads to a sense of helplessness and hopelessness, where the child cannot control their life or make positive changes. This sense of helplessness can be incredibly damaging to the development of negativity.

Finally, parent comments can undermine a child's sense of independence and control. When parents are overly critical or controlling of their child's decisions and actions, it can lead to the child feeling like they have no authority over their own life. Increasing feelings of frustration, aggravation, and distress. Parents need to be mindful of their words when communicating with their children and strive to be supportive, validating, and encouraging. By creating a supportive environment, parents can better their children by developing a strong sense of self-worth and resilience, reducing their risk of depression.

Parents need to remember their childhood experiences while trying to find balance in creating the best possible outcome for their children. It's a delicate act that can be achieved with patience, love, and understanding. Remembering the joys and challenges of our upbringing can help guide us as we navigate the ups and downs of parenthood. If someone is feeling helpless at school, nobody needs the same feelings at home.

Contact your grandparents or your best friend's parents in case of parent issues. Wisdom is everywhere you look. Use those communication skills and ask for assistance. So many parents will blame the internet for teen issues. And the reality is the internet doesn't help make matters any better, just like bad parenting. Not everyone has perfect parents, and there are no perfect children. Many of us are broken in some way, shape, or form, and we should be able to admit we all can become better people and improve.

Smartphone Addiction and Depression

In our increasingly digital world, smartphones have become nearly inseparable from our daily lives. They serve as tools for entertainment, navigation, communication, education, and even as our personal assistants. However, excessive use of these devices, especially among teenagers, can lead to behavioral addiction, known as smartphone addiction. This type of addiction has been linked to a few mental health issues, including separation anxiety and mental breakdowns.

Smartphone addiction, called nomophobia, is characterized by an excessive reliance on these electronics, leading to problematic behaviors. These might include the inability to reduce using the device and experiencing anxiety or distress when the phone is unavailable. The constant connectivity and the social pressures often accompanying smartphone use can exacerbate anxiety and depression. Furthermore, excessive use can interfere with sleep, contribute to lower physical activity levels, and decrease face-to-face social interactions, all of which can adversely impact mental health.

Research has suggested a significant correlation between excessive smartphone use and increased symptoms of depression among teenagers. There are several reasons why this might be the case. Firstly, using smartphones, particularly late at night, can interfere with sleep. Teenagers who stay up late using their phones may experience reduced sleep quality and quantity, contributing to mood disorders, including depression. It could be that those with depression are more likely to use smartphones excessively as escapism.

In the 1980s and 1990s, people relied less on technology and more on their brains to remember things. In those eras, it was common for people to remember phone numbers, addresses, and important dates. This helped improve memory and cognitive skills and encouraged face-to-face interactions as people had to rely on their social networks to remember important information.

Nowadays, we rely on expensive equipment to store and retrieve information, but it's essential to remember that our brains are powerful tools that must be exercised regularly. Challenging ourselves to remember crucial details without relying on technology can keep our brains sharp and improve our overall cognitive function. Living in a more accessible world doesn't equate to existing in a conscious setting. Recognizing the potential risks associated with excessive smartphone use is crucial in raising awareness and prompting discussions about healthy technology use.

When it comes to the mind, you'll lose your memory bank and become mentally lazy if you don't practice memorization. Reducing screen time and promoting healthier habits can help mitigate adverse mental health effects. Here are some strategies teenagers and their parents or caregivers can adopt:

Set Boundaries: Implement designated times for electronics and periods when equipment is off-limits, such as during meals or an hour before bed.

Digital Detox: Encourage regular breaks from smartphones. This could involve spending a whole day without using the device or shorter, more frequent periods throughout the day.

Mindful Usage: Encourage teens to question their usage. Is it purposeful or mindless? Do they feel better or worse after using their device? Being mindful of smartphone use can help teens identify unhealthy patterns and triggers. The brain wants to be entertained; it shouldn't always involve an electronic device.

Alternative Activities: Promote outdoor activities, reading, board and card games, and spending time with friends and family.

Chapter Five

Dangers of Recklessness

When venturing on the challenging journey of understanding and dealing with teen depression, it's crucial to recognize some of its darker manifestations. Recklessness and violence, while not as commonly discussed as sadness or withdrawal, can sometimes surface as signs of a deeper struggle with mental health. This chapter aims to shed light on these less-discussed yet potentially devastating behaviors, giving us insight into their relationship with teenage depression.

This chapter explores understanding reckless behavior. This can be anything from small, harmless risks to actions that can harm oneself. Following that, we'll explore the link between violence and depression, which can be distressing but is nonetheless important to discuss. As we navigate these challenging issues, remember that knowledge is power, and understanding these behaviors is the first step towards finding ways to cope with them effectively.

Understanding Reckless Behavior

Reckless behavior in depressed teens involves dissecting the complex web of feelings and motivations that may lead a teenager to engage in risky actions. This recklessness can be present in various ways and may indicate deeper psychological struggles. Reckless behavior is engaging in actions that put oneself or others at unnecessary risk. These behaviors can range from skipping school, engaging in substance use, and driving dangerously to participating in risky sexual activities.

This reckless behavior may serve as a coping mechanism for dealing with overwhelming negative emotions, creating a dangerous cycle of risk and relief for teenagers. When experiencing depression, teens may feel trapped in a world of negativity, despair, emotional pain, and boredom. As a result, some may resort to reckless behavior as an escape or a cry for help. This may bring about a temporary relief or distraction from the emotional turmoil they're experiencing. It's a risky and unhealthy coping mechanism, potentially leading to severe consequences that can affect their health, academic performance, and relationships.

Impulsivity plays a crucial role in reckless behavior among teens. The teenage brain is still developing, and the area responsible for impulse control, the prefrontal cortex, fully matures at the age of 26. Depression can further impair impulse control, leading to a higher propensity for reckless behavior. In more severe cases, recklessness can extend to self-harm and suicidal ideation, some of the most alarming manifestations of teenage depression. While not all teenagers who engage in reckless behaviors are suicidal, increasing such behaviors can be a red flag that the individual is struggling significantly and needs immediate help.

Being aware of the signs of reckless behavior can help identify teens who may be struggling with depression. Sudden changes in behavior, such as increased substance use, a disregard for safety, or neglect of responsibilities, can signal that a teenager is engaging in reckless behavior. Understanding reckless behavior in depressed teens is not about placing blame or inciting fear but rather about fostering awareness, empathy, and proactive intervention.

This understanding equips us to better support teenagers who might be struggling and guide them toward healthier coping mechanisms. In the following sections, we'll explore these strategies and discuss how to address and reduce teen reckless conduct. Irresponsible behavior can appear in numerous ways, varying in severity and impact. Some examples might include:

Substance Abuse: Using drugs or alcohol is reckless. Substance use poses health risks and can impact a teen's life in numerous other ways, affecting academic performance and relationships and possibly leading to legal trouble. If a teenager is caught with drugs, it can lead to severe consequences.

Depending on the severity of the offense and the type of drug involved, the consequences can range from a warning or probation to fines, community service, and even jail time. Furthermore, a drug conviction can have long-lasting effects on your future, including difficulty finding employment, obtaining financial aid for college, and even getting a driver's license. It's crucial for teenagers to understand the risks and potential consequences of drug use and to make intelligent choices to avoid putting themselves in harm's way.

Dangerous Driving: Anytime you drive, the risks and potential consequences are severe. Whether it's speeding, drunk driving, or ignoring traffic rules, these actions can put others on the road in great danger. Teenagers must realize their efforts can have serious consequences, including injury or death. This is why it's essential to always follow the laws of the road and drive responsibly.

It's not worth risking your life or the lives of others for a few moments of reckless behavior. If nonsense occurs, call a taxi or call your parents; anything is better than facing more challenging problems. There are enough troubles in life; nobody needs to increase household stress. It's better to get a butt chewing from your family than the alternate course.

Risky Sexual Behavior: Engaging in unprotected sex or having multiple sexual partners can lead to sexually transmitted diseases and unplanned pregnancies. One million teens each year are having children, altering their life course. There's nothing wrong with God's precious children, but individuals shouldn't base their decisions on a good time. Grab a Bible and read 1 Corinthians 3:16–18. You're a temple for your spirit; treat temples with care and your body respectfully. Don't deceive yourself; examine your actions so you can become wise.

Neglect of Responsibilities: This could involve skipping school, failing to complete assignments, or ignoring home and work duties. Everything in life is a building block. The more you accomplish, the better your preparation will be. One day, you'll be an adult taking care of business. Failure to learn and take ownership of tasks will leave you completely overwhelmed later in your years.

Schoolwork keeps your brain growing and learning new things with a healthy pressure of assignments. Everyone eventually returns home to handle dishes, trash, laundry, cleaning up, and putting stuff away. Get involved in your own life; otherwise, everything you're surrounded with will be overwhelming, bringing new complexities. It's always better to face obstacles head-on and complete your tasks as they come rather than wait-ing until the last second to handle everything. By staying on top of your responsibilities, you can avoid feeling overwhelmed by ensuring everything is promptly addressed.

Physical Risk-Taking: This could involve activities like extreme sports without proper safety measures, physical fights, or any other action that puts one's physical health at immediate risk. Do your best to play smart. Fights are not always avoidable! Do your best to de-escalate the problems and find assistance. Joining martial arts is truly the best experience you'll ever have. Develop mental stability, learn self-defense, and learn how to keep your mind positive.

In defining reckless behavior, it's important to remember that some risk-taking is normal in adolescence and human nature; there's a clear difference between healthy risk-taking and recklessness.

Since depression can lead to unknown feelings and emotions, a teen might turn to reckless behavior to escape or relieve these sensations. This can temporarily distract them from the emotional turmoil, a fleeting mo-ment of excitement, or a sense of control over their life. Here are some ways in which reckless behavior can act as a coping mechanism.

Adrenaline Rush: Engaging in dangerous activities can trigger an adrenaline rush, which might momentarily distract teenagers from their depressive feelings. This adrenaline-induced high can become a form of escape, making the risk-taking behavior seem appealing.

Seeking Validation: Some teenagers might engage in reckless behavior to seek peer validation. The desire to fit in or be accepted can lead them to take actions they might not otherwise consider.

A Cry for Help: Sometimes, reckless behavior can be a silent cry for help. Teens might hope that someone notices their dangerous actions and helps.

Self-Punishment: In more severe cases, reckless behavior can serve as a form of self-punishment, reflecting deep feelings of self-loathing or worthlessness often associated with depression.

Understanding reckless behavior as a coping mechanism for depression can help adults approach this issue with empathy and compassion. However, it's vital to note that while this understanding explains the behavior, it does not excuse it.

The Role of Impulsivity

The teen brain is going through major changes and rewiring, especially in the prefrontal cortex. This area oversees decision-making, controlling impulses, and thinking about the future. Impulsivity is a key factor contributing to reckless behavior among teenagers. However, this brain area does not fully mature until the mid-20s, making teenagers more susceptible to impulsive actions.

Impaired Decision-Making: Each person hopefully considers the pros and cons of decisions, potential risks, and rewards while thinking about long-term consequences. In depressed teens, this region is degraded or compromised due to the impact of the depressive symptoms, leading to impaired decision-making abilities. They may struggle to think through the potential consequences of their actions, resulting in sudden and risky behavior.

Heightened Emotional Reactivity: Teenagers are known for their emotional volatility, which can be further amplified in individuals with depression. Intense emotions can overwhelm their ability to regulate impulses, as the vibrant centers of the brain exert a more substantial influence on behavior. This emotional reactivity and depressive feelings can push a teenager toward engaging in reckless behavior as an impulsive reaction to intense negative emotions.

Immediate Gratification: Depressed teens may seek immediate relief from their emotional pain, and engaging in reckless behavior can provide a temporary escape or a surge of excitement. The desire for immediate gratification may override their ability to consider the potential long-term consequences or risks associated with their actions.

Sensation-Seeking: Some depressed teenagers may engage in reckless behavior to seek excitement or stimulation. They may feel a sense of numbness or emptiness due to their depression and turn to risky actions to experience a rush of adrenaline or intense emotions.

Understanding the role of impulsivity in reckless behavior is crucial in addressing the underlying factors contributing to such actions. It highlights the need for targeted interventions that focus on developing healthy coping strategies, enhancing decision-making skills, and strengthening impulse control.

The Link of Violence

Not all depressed individuals engage in violent behavior. Aggression refers to a range of behaviors intended to cause harm or injury, whether physical, verbal, or psychological. Violence, on the other hand, typically refers to more extreme forms of physical aggression that cause harm or injury to others. Both aggression and violence can manifest in various ways, from verbal threats to physical altercations.

As a teenager, the world can be a confusing and stressful place. Between the pressures of school, relationships, and figuring out who you are, it's no wonder many teenagers struggle with depression. Unfortunately, depression can be linked to violence, creating a dangerous situation for teenagers and those around them. There are a few different ways that depression and violence can be connected in teenagers.

One of the most common is using drugs and alcohol. Many teenagers turn to these substances to cope with their depression, but they can also make them more prone to violence. Drugs and alcohol impair judgment and make it more difficult for teenagers to control their impulses, leading to violent behavior. Another way that depression and violence can be linked is through a lack of social support.

When teenagers feel isolated and alone, they can quickly become angry and lash out at others. This is especially true if they are dealing with bullying or other forms of abuse. Without a support system, it can be difficult for teenagers to manage their emotions and avoid violence. Depression can also be linked to violence in teenagers who have experienced trauma. Traumatic events like neglect or abuse can profoundly impact a teenager's mental health. They may struggle with feelings of anger, fear, and anxiety, which can lead to violent outbursts.

Additionally, trauma can impact a teenager's ability to form healthy relationships, making managing their emotions and avoiding violence more challenging. This might mean seeking therapy or counseling, providing a safe and supportive environment, or helping teenagers find alternate ways to deal with their emotions.

Several factors contribute to the manifestation of violent behavior in depressed teenagers. It's essential to recognize that these factors are not definitive causes but rather potential influences that interact with an individual's unique circumstances:

Intense Emotions and Anger: Depression often manifests in intense and overwhelming emotions, including anger and irritability. For some teenagers, these emotions can escalate to the point where they express their distress through violent behavior.

Feelings of Hopelessness and Desperation: Prolonged feelings of hopelessness and despair, common in depression, can lead to a distorted worldview, where violence may be perceived as a means of release or control.

Co-Occurring Mental Health Conditions: Depression can accompany mental health conditions, such as anxiety or conduct disorder, which can further increase the risk of violent behavior.

Substance Abuse: The influence of friends with drugs or alcohol impairs our judgment and increases the likelihood of engaging in violent acts.

Recognize that violence is not a healthy or effective means of seeking support, and intervention should be focused on addressing the underlying issues while providing appropriate professional assistance. Breaking the cycle of violence and depression requires a multifaceted approach that addresses both mental health and the factors contributing to aggression. It is crucial to ensure the safety of all individuals involved while providing support and resources to those struggling with depression. Strategies may include:

Mental Health Treatment: Effective treatment for depression, including therapy and medication, could help individuals manage their symptoms, reduce aggressive tendencies, and develop healthy coping mechanisms.

Anger Management and Conflict Resolution: Teaching healthy ways to manage anger and resolve conflicts can empower teenagers to express their emotions in non-violent ways and foster more beneficial relationships.

Intervention: Encouraging a healthy network of family members, good friends, and professionals who can provide guidance, understanding, and intervention is crucial in addressing violence and depression.

Education and Awareness: Promoting awareness about the link between violence and depression can help reduce stigma, increase empathy, and ensure early detection and intervention.

Overall, the link between violence and depression in teenagers is complex and requires careful attention and support. By understanding the underlying factors that can contribute to violent behavior, we can work to create a safe and compassionate environment for all teenagers. Whether it's through therapy, social support, or other forms of intervention, there are many ways that we can help teenagers manage their emotions.

You need to fight the war within yourself to change your life. It's hard to take responsibility, but you must learn new things. You may feel uncomfortable, and this discomfort is how we grow. That's how we become strong. You will always be weak if you run away from despair and resistance your whole life.

If you want to grow, you must make friends with your pain by embracing discomfort and enjoying the struggle. It's not easy to look in the mirror and change your life. Don't speak negatively about yourself; your body doesn't know the difference. If you prime yourself for negativity, you'll absorb those thoughts if you poison your mind.

Change the way you talk to yourself. What are you not changing? Are you choosing to stay where you are? Remember, in your weakest moments, the strongest version of you is waiting to launch, but if you have no pressure, you'll have no diamonds. The world's best people have come from dealing with problems and handling personal struggles.

Chapter Six

Understanding Intrusive Thoughts

E very person, regardless of age, experiences intrusive thoughts. These are thoughts that pop up out of nowhere and won't go away. For instance, a catchy song you heard on the radio that has been playing on repeat in your mind all day. While these thoughts can be mildly annoying, they are usually relatively harmless. The primary characteristic of these annoyances is their profound impact on your quality of life.

They can be more like a pebble in your shoe or increase to a boulder blocking your path. It's essential to realize that these irritating thoughts are normal in human cognition. If you are battling these thoughts, don't worry; it doesn't necessarily mean anything. The mind loves to be entertained. Whether you re-visit a funny movie or song from another day or replay a terrible moment in your life, don't fret; the brain loves pulling information and ideas from anywhere.

If anyone would like to learn more about intrusive thoughts, a great resource is my book called -

Combat Intrusive Thoughts
How to Overcome the Eight Troublesome Mindsets
and Disturbing Mentalities

The good news is that these thoughts usually dissipate independently with time. Just like that song eventually gets replaced by another tune, these thoughts tend to fade away. However, if you're finding it hard to shake them off, simple techniques such as distraction or mindfulness exercises can be beneficial. By focusing on something else or training your mind to stay in the present, you can often 'switch the channel' and rid yourself of the irritating thought.

One way to deal with these thoughts is through self-soothing exercises such as deep breathing, cleaning the house, doing a hobby, or even taking a walk outdoors. Such activities not only distract the mind but also help in promoting overall well-being.

Thoughts are typically characterized by their unwelcome nature. They can range from slightly disturbing to deeply distressing and could cause significant anxiety, especially when they become persistent. These thoughts may revolve around various themes, including harm, doubt, violence, sex, and religion. Intrusive thoughts are common in everyone, most notably those with obsessive-compulsive disorder and those who feel stressed out.

In the grand orchestra of the human body, the mind is the maestro, directing the symphony of thoughts, feelings, and actions that make us who we are. We often consider the mind an invincible fortress able to weather any storm. However, the truth is that our minds, much like the rest of our bodies, have limits. They can be influenced, shaped, and sometimes overwhelmed by our experiences.

Consider, for instance, the case of intrusive thoughts. These are instances where the mind, under specific circumstances, manifests patterns that can be distressing and disruptive. Repetitive thoughts, impulses, or mental images can become intrusive and unwanted. This is not to say that our minds are weak or defective; far from it. What it does suggest, however, is that our minds are susceptible, malleable, and sensitive to both internal and external influences. Life experiences, genetic predispositions, and biochemical imbalances can all affect the mind's functionality, leading to violence and depression.

Knowing this can help reframe our understanding and approach to mental health. Mental health issues are not personal failings or lack of willpower. They result from complex interactions between various factors, much like any other health condition. Acknowledging that our minds are not as invincible as we'd like opens the door to understanding, empathy, and effective intervention.

Understanding the nature of our minds also empowers us to seek help. Recognizing that mental health conditions are legitimate health issues, not just a matter of 'snapping out of it,' can be the first step in the healing journey. Whether talking to a trusted friend, seeking professional help, or joining a support group – reaching out can make a world of difference.

Coping with intrusive thoughts involves recognizing the vulnerability of our minds and taking steps to care for them. These are not quick fixes but steady, gradual steps towards gaining control over your mental landscape. It's true that our minds may not be as impervious to mental health issues as we once believed. But our minds are indeed formidable regarding resilience, adaptability, and the capacity for change. And with the proper knowledge, tools, and support, we can harness this potential to manage intrusive thoughts effectively.

Understanding this balance and acknowledging the vulnerability of our minds while harnessing resilience is a crucial aspect of navigating life with anger or depression. It paves the way for empathy, understanding, and practical strategies for coping with intrusive thoughts and compulsive behaviors.

It's worth noting that intrusive thoughts, in themselves, don't define our character or intentions. They do not reflect who we are or what we truly want. In fact, they often represent what we fear the most, which is why they cause so much distress. Recognizing the origins of intrusive thoughts is an essential step toward understanding and managing them.

This knowledge can aid in demystifying these thoughts, reducing the fear and stigma around them, and providing a solid foundation for developing effective coping strategies. Remember, the goal isn't to stop these thoughts completely; that's nearly impossible, but rather to change how we react to them, ultimately reducing their impact on our lives. These thoughts are symptoms of stress, anxiety, and challenges. Coming to terms with this recognition can be difficult, as people who carry heavy burdens often keep their emotions to themselves.

It's natural to feel conflicted when you realize your thoughts are unusual. Although it can bring a sense of relief and validation, it can also present challenges. Remember that you're not at fault for experiencing these thoughts. Your mindset is your most significant asset. It's common to have doubts or uncertainties about the nature of your thoughts, especially if they are intrusive and persistent.

Acknowledging this difference and recognizing that they may not align with your typical thinking patterns can be a crucial aspect of understanding what's going on in your mind. In some cases, examining your old mentalities and thought patterns can help you find new avenues for positive corrections. By reflecting on your past experiences and thought processes, you can identify triggers or habits contributing to your intrusive thoughts. This self-reflection can provide insights into your behavior and help you develop strategies for managing your thoughts and emotions.

Understanding Suicide

Comments are often overlooked or misunderstood; one of these signs is making off-hand comments or jokes about suicide. Taking these comments seriously is essential, as they could be a cry for help. Firstly, we need to understand why teenagers might joke about suicide. It's a complex issue, and the reasons behind it can be just as intricate.

Often, these jokes or off-hand comments are a way for teens to communicate their pain without directly stating their intentions or feelings. It's their way of reaching out and testing the waters to see how others might respond if they share their true feelings. Firstly, it's essential not to dismiss or laugh off these comments, even if they're presented as a joke. Do not judge or criticize them for such remarks; remember, these could be their way of reaching out or expressing their distress.

For some, humor is a coping mechanism. Making light of their darkest thoughts might be a way for them to manage their emotions and deal with their depression. Sometimes, making jokes about suicide may be a misguided attempt to normalize what they felt or thought during certain depressing moments. Teens might make direct statements like, "I wish I were dead," or indirect comments such as, "You won't have to worry about me much longer." They might also say things about suicide or frequently reference it in conversation.

If a teen starts giving away prized possessions, writing goodbye letters, or suddenly seems happier or calmer after a period of depression, it might indicate they're considering suicide. Pay attention to their social media posts. They might share posts about feeling hopeless, trapped, or being a burden to others. Navigating conversations around suicide can feel daunting. The gravity of the situation can leave us unsure about what to say or how to react. Either way, get them help immediately.

The mind could have thoughts of getting even with someone or just wandering off. These thoughts are a part of the brain using its creativity and imagination. Usually, the thoughts everyone possesses don't go anywhere other than irritation, aggravation, or something funny. But if you're depressed, the mind might create images of something to stop the discomfort of depression.

It doesn't mean anyone will go through it, but a teen doesn't know any better. They'll talk about it, thinking it was their idea without realizing it's just the unlimited imagination taking off with ideas either wanted or unwanted.

University textbooks are often based on years of research on various topics. These books are frequently reused, edited, and launched as a new edition and suggest that people with intrusive thoughts are uncommon. However, no one wants to admit to having an imagination or conscience that might lead to alternative ways of thinking. The truth is everyone experiences intrusive thoughts to some degree, and it's the intensity of these thoughts that varies.

Chapter Seven

Physical Manifestations

D epression doesn't only impact an individual's mental and emotional state; it can also lead to various physical symptoms that may not be immediately recognized as being connected to depression. In this chapter, we will explore these physical manifestations that are often associated with depression in teenagers. Understanding these physical signs is a crucial component of recognizing and responding to depression, as they provide a more comprehensive picture of what the teenager might be experiencing.

Teenagers struggling with depression might exhibit changes in their eating and sleeping patterns, increased levels of anger, or unexplained aches and pains. Each symptom provides a piece of the puzzle, contributing to our understanding of the complexities of teenage depression. Through this chapter, I hope to shed light on these multi-faceted symptoms, fostering a greater understanding of the nature of depression. There's an abundance of things that can hinder every part of our being. Many people are falling to pieces from the inside out.

Shifts in Eating and Sleeping

One of the physical manifestations that are often observed among teenagers is a change in their eating and sleeping patterns. These shifts might seem unpredictable or unusual, but they're frequently linked to the emotional turmoil that depression can cause. These changes in fundamental daily routines can further exacerbate depressive symptoms, leading to a vicious cycle that's hard to break.

To provide a deeper understanding of this issue, I'll break it down into two main sections: eating patterns and sleeping patterns. The relationship between changes in appetite can manifest in two primary ways:

Overeating: Some teens may turn to food for comfort when they're feeling depressed, leading to overeating or binge eating. This can often result in weight gain, affecting their self-esteem and worsening depression.

Loss of Appetite: On the other hand, some teenagers may lose their appetite entirely when depressed. They might skip meals or eat very little, leading to weight loss and physical weakness.

Similar to eating patterns, shifts in sleeping patterns can also be a common physical manifestation of depression. Teenagers might deal with insomnia, hypersomnia, or disturbed sleep:

Insomnia: A common symptom of depression where individuals have trouble falling or staying asleep. Lack of quality sleep can make it harder to manage and recover from depression, leading to a perpetuating cycle.

Hypersomnia: Some may experience hypersomnia, which involves excessive sleepiness. They might find themselves sleeping for extended periods yet still feeling tired and lacking energy during their waking hours.

Disturbed Sleep: Depressed teenagers might also experience awakenings during the night, nightmares, or restless sleep. Addressing changes in sleeping patterns can significantly contribute to managing depression. Some strategies include:

Mindful Eating: Mindful eating involves paying close attention to hunger and fullness cues, appreciating the taste and texture of food, and recognizing emotional triggers for overeating or undereating. By practicing mindful eating, teenagers can start to rebuild a healthy relationship with food.

Balanced Diet: Encouraging a balanced diet rich in fruits, vegetables, protein shakes, lean proteins, and whole grains can help stabilize mood.

Sleep Hygiene: Good sleep hygiene involves practices that help promote quality sleep, such as taking a nice shower before bed to relax the body, maintaining a consistent sleep schedule, creating a peaceful sleep environment, and avoiding screens before bed.

Mindful Relaxation Techniques: Techniques like deep breathing exercises, progressive muscle relaxation, stretching, and listening to nature music can help relax the mind and body, facilitating better sleep.

It's important to remember that eating and sleeping patterns are interconnected. For example, sleeping issues can disrupt the hormones that control normal hunger and fullness feelings, leading to overeating or poor food choices. Similarly, eating large meals late at night can disrupt sleep. Therefore, simultaneously addressing both areas can be more effective in managing depressive symptoms.

In the end, acknowledging and understanding these unpredictable shifts in eating and sleeping patterns can be the first step in helping teenagers navigate depression. Both parents and teenagers should understand that these physical changes are part of the broader picture of depression and that addressing them can contribute to a better quality of life and improved mental health.

Anger and Unknown Aches and Pains

We can understand depression is commonly associated with unhappiness, sorrow, and a lack of interest or pleasure in activities. However, it can also manifest in less obvious ways, such as increased irritability or anger and physical aches and pains. While we often imagine depression as creating feelings of profound sadness or apathy, a common manifestation for many, especially teenagers, can be increased irritability or anger.

Understanding this connection can give us a more nuanced picture of how depression can present itself. Feelings of frustration, disappointment, and injustice can build up, leading to increased irritability or explosive anger. This anger is often a mask for the underlying emotions of helplessness and hopelessness that characterize depression. Recognizing the signs of anger can vary, but they often involve a low frustration tolerance, overreactions to minor annoyances, and resentment. It's important to note that everyone has bad days or moments of frustration, but when these moments become more frequent or intense, it could be a sign of an underlying issue.

It's a complex interplay of social, psychological, and biological factors. It manifests in the form of physical symptoms that may be difficult to diagnose, such as unexplained aches and pains. Depression can make physical pain feel more intense than it actually is. Both physical pain and depression involve the same neurotransmitters and neural pathways in the brain. Shared pathways can amplify the experience of pain when depression sets in.

These physical symptoms can include headaches, stomachaches, back pain, or general body aches. While these occur for various reasons, if they persist without a clear cause, it's probably from the depression you're feeling. Recognizing that depression can cause anger, physical pain, and sadness is crucial for effective treatment. Suppose you or a teenager are dealing with persistent anger or unexplained physical aches and pains alongside other depressive symptoms. In that case, various strategies can be implemented to help manage these symptoms. These strategies can help manage the physical symptoms:

Physical Activity: Regular outdoor activities have been shown to help reduce symptoms of depression and alleviate certain types of physical pain. Even low-intensity activities such as walking can be beneficial.

Mind-body Techniques: Meditation, martial arts, or tai chi can help teens connect their minds and bodies, potentially reducing physical pain and promoting relaxation. When you exercise or do light stretching, your body releases endorphins, which are natural mood boosters. Incorporating regular physical activity into your routine can help your body remove depression and improve pain and joint pain. In the same way, when someone gets a knee replacement, the doctors will say, keep moving around. Sitting around waiting for something to magically happen isn't the answer.

Chapter Eight

Eating Disorders

O bviously, we need to eat to survive; humans cannot survive without food. However, abnormal eating behaviors such as binge eating or purging can cause severe personal and socioeconomic problems. Food is often associated with significant emotional responses in people. It also plays a fundamental role in the soul of our physical and psychological makeup.

Eating disorders adversely influence the body's life cycle due to the dysfunctional relationship between the mind and body. As a result, overconsumption is an additional strain on the body's physiological and metabolic systems, which can cause serious health problems. Overeating and depression can frequently coexist. Individuals may overeat to cope with their negative emotions and feelings of hopelessness. They may turn to food for comfort or to numb their pain, leading to binge eating and weight gain.

Additionally, depression can affect a teen's appetite and metabolism, making them more prone to overeating and unhealthy food choices. As a result, parents and caregivers need to monitor their teen's eating habits. These three disorders influence each other by increasing the emotional instability of the person suffering from one or both conditions.

Anorexia, Binge-eating and Bulimia

The connection between anorexia and depression is solid. Anorexia is a psychological state that involves unhealthy control over food intake. Anorexia often begins in adolescence and usually affects young women. People living with Anorexia may see themselves as overweight despite being underweight or even dangerously thin. They attach great importance to their weight, constantly preoccupied with food and its effects on their bodies.

Anorexics tend to avoid eating for fear of gaining weight or because they believe that food has no taste or tastes horrible. However, these teenagers tend to consume vast amounts of food at mealtimes and repeatedly attempt to become thinner through unhealthy dieting, excessive exercise, vomiting after meals, or taking laxatives or diuretics.

They may also participate in extreme sports to burn off calories or even refuse to eat due to the fear that their bodies will change. The anorexic's inability to see their natural weight may be connected to various psychological issues and can result from an attempt to gain control over oneself and one's surroundings. Anorexia has a very high rate of mortality. Anorexia sufferers are at higher risk for heart disease, osteoporosis, infertility, kidney failure, low blood pressure, muscle loss, and osteoporosis.

Teenagers with depression are often at higher risk for the onset of anorexia than teenagers without depression. They tend to engage in extreme dieting and other behaviors that promote anorexia, such as excessive exercise. Adolescents with depression are also more likely to attempt suicide when displaying symptoms of anorexia than adolescents who have other eating disorders. The presence of anorexia in depressed teens can be problematic. Depression can interfere with the ability to take care of oneself and may result in death from anorexia. It's also associated with many other health consequences, such as muscle loss and impaired quality of life.

Binge-eating, like anorexia, is another mental illness related to depression among teens. It's dangerous, accompanied by feelings of guilt and shame after a binge-eating episode. These episodes can occur as often as once, twice a week, or more frequently. These episodes involve consuming much food quickly, often within two hours. People can eat a considerable amount of food during the episode, and a feeling of loss of control follows the food consumption. The disorder often causes severe health problems, including obesity, high blood pressure, heart disease, gallbladder disease, diabetes, osteoarthritis, and breathing problems.

It can also cause other mental health issues among depressed teenagers, such as anxiety disorders, social phobia, drug abuse, excessive drinking, or other actions that aim to cope with depression, like regurgitation or laxative abuse. Teenagers are more vulnerable to developing binge eating. For example, teens are often overly concerned about their weight and food choices. They may also engage in binging for self-comfort or self-medication for stress, anxiety, anger, or even low mood.

Adolescents diagnosed with any depressive condition are at a higher risk of developing binge-eating disorder, with an estimated 1% of patients suffering from this condition. The disorder is marked by frequent and intense binges and an increased occurrence of binge-eating episodes.

Bulimia is defined as episodes of inappropriate and extreme weight control three or more times a week for at least one month. These episodes are followed by feelings of guilt about their eating behavior and can result in significant weight loss. Typically, it begins during adolescence or early adulthood. Bulimia frequently involves binge eating, followed by purging through vomiting, laxatives, or diuretics to prevent weight gain. Purging often results in significant weight loss and other related health problems.

Depressed teens are more likely to develop bulimia than teenagers without depression. These teens are also more susceptible to developing binge-eating and anorexia nervosa. Bulimia is associated with various psychological and emotional problems, including high anxiety levels, low self-esteem, and a fear of gaining weight. Bulimia may help the teenager cope with such feelings or simulate control or comfort in a trying situation. But it'll reinforce a negative body image and promote further self-destructive behavior.

Teenagers are often in a bad position. They usually don't know what's happening to their bodies. They may be uncertain whether they're attractive or average in appearance and may feel alone with their problems. What's more troubling is that eating disorders have many severe physical consequences, both immediate and long-term. Such effects include dehydration, nutrient deficiency, vitamin deficiencies, slowed growth rate or weight loss due to inadequate food intake, electrolyte imbalances, low blood sodium levels, and heart failure.

Not surprisingly, teenagers with depression who develop an eating disorder are at higher risk of attempting suicide than depressed teenagers without an eating disorder. This risk is mainly present in teenagers with bulimia, as up to 3% of patients with bulimia desire death. In addition, the risk of death by suicide is also elevated among family members or people close to individuals with severe eating disorders.

Adolescence, characterized by swift physical and emotional transformation, can pose significant challenges. Teenagers grappling with eating disorders and depression may find it particularly difficult to effectively manage these rapid changes, such as throat and stomach ulcers, tooth decay and cavities, esophagus inflammation, damage to your intestines, and stomach lining damage. Before recognizing that something is wrong, some teenagers may respond impulsively, leading to potentially harmful behaviors. For instance, they might avoid social gatherings, such as parties or barbecues, to hide their struggles, leading to further emotional distress and a deepening sense of loneliness.

Chapter Nine

Psychological Factors

P sychological factors can affect how people see themselves and feel about their bodies. Understanding how these factors work together is crucial to addressing these issues effectively. We can develop healthier strategies to prevent negative self-perception. Teenagers often struggle with these issues, and identifying and addressing the underlying psychological factors can help improve treatment.

These factors can impact an individual's self-image, emotions, beliefs, and behaviors, and their interaction with biological, social, and environmental factors can create complex dynamics. Tailored interventions can help teenagers navigate these challenges.

Low self-esteem is one of the most important psychological factors contributing to eating disorders. Self-esteem, or self-worth, refers to an individual's general view of themselves. It's a judgment about oneself based on one's characteristics and achievements in comparison with the expectations of others. Each teen is trying to escape or distract themselves from their depression.

Psychological influences such as one's family upbringing, social experiences, and emotional state can affect a teenager's sense of self and impact the development of disordered eating behaviors. For example, when teenagers experience adversity during childhood, such as growing up in a dysfunctional home and not feeling adequate, they are at higher risk for developing low self-esteem. Adolescents who grow up in families exposed to harsh criticism and bullying have increased chances of developing bulimia nervosa or binge eating disorder. Adolescents who experience abuse or neglect are at increased risk for developing an eating disorder.

Overcoming obstacles is an essential part of life. It's through these challenges that we learn and grow, becoming stronger and more resilient. There are many different types of obstacles that we may encounter, whether they be physical, mental, emotional, or spiritual. Whatever the barrier, we must remember that we have the power to overcome it. One of the keys to overcoming obstacles is to have a positive attitude.

When we approach challenges with an optimistic mindset, regroup our thoughts, and focus on how we can make a difference by making an impact, we will find solutions and overcome the obstacle that stands in our way. Be persistent and never give up. Even if we encounter setbacks and failures, we must keep pushing forward and keep sight of our goals.

Seek help and support from others. We all need a helping hand occasionally, and there is no shame in asking for help. Whether it be a friend, family member, or professional, find something you want to accomplish, make it happen, and celebrate small victories until you increase your self-worth.

Body Image

Another important factor contributing to eating disorders is body image concerns This refers to a distorted, harmful, or disordered way of thinking about one's physical appearance and body. It can be defined as a person's perception of their physical attributes and those of others, such as appearance, shape, weight, or size. Increased body image concerns may lead to poor self-esteem and a negative perception of one's body image, which can cause feelings of shame.

This can intensify a teenager's desire to lose weight and engage in eating disorders to lose weight or feel better about oneself. Teenagers navigating the world of advertising and body weight image can be challenging. With so many ads and messages bombarding us daily, it's easy to feel overwhelmed and uncertain of ourselves. However, there are steps we can take to help us battle these messages and overcome the issues they may cause.

One of the first things we can do is be aware of how ads and media can manipulate our perceptions of ourselves and our bodies. When we see images of models and celebrities with seemingly perfect bodies, we must remind ourselves that these images are often heavily edited and do not reflect reality. We can also seek out more diverse and realistic representations of bodies in media and advertising to counteract the narrow and unrealistic beauty standards that are often promoted.

Another powerful tool is to build our self-esteem and confidence so we are less susceptible to negative messaging about our bodies. This can involve engaging in positive self-talk, setting realistic goals for ourselves, and cultivating a strong support system of friends and family who encourage and uplift us. Finally, it's important to remember that our worth as human beings is not determined by our body weight or appearance.

We are so much more than our physical bodies, and we should strive to focus on our talents, passions, and inner qualities as much as possible. By keeping these strategies in mind, we can take control of our perceptions of ourselves and overcome the adverse effects of advertising and body weight image.

Identity

Certain aspects of identity, such as ethnic background, socioeconomic status, gender, sexual orientation, religion, and physical appearance, play roles in developing ourselves for the future. Believing in your identity as a teenager is crucial to becoming a better person. One way to do this is by reflecting on your values, interests, and experiences to better understand who you are.

Identifying your passions and pursuing activities that align with them can help you build confidence and a sense of purpose. It's also important to surround yourself with positive influences and seek out supportive relationships with friends and family members who accept and appreciate you for who you are.

Finally, practicing self-care and prioritizing your mental and physical health can help you feel more grounded and confident in your identity. Remember, you are unique and valuable just the way you are, and there is no one-size-fits-all definition of what it means to be a "better" person.

Emotional Regulation Difficulties

Difficulties in regulating emotions, such as managing stress, coping with negative feelings, or dealing with interpersonal conflicts, are always on the front line. Some individuals may turn to disorderly eating patterns as a maladaptive coping mechanism to numb emotions, gain control, or find comfort. Regulate your emotions without feeling overwhelmed by practicing mindfulness. This involves becoming more aware of your feelings and thoughts without judging or responding.

Incorporating mindful techniques into your daily routine, such as engaging in deep breathing exercises, practicing meditation, and taking time to reflect on what is causing you distress and whether it's worth worrying about, can assist in remaining composed and grounded in the present. Finding healthy ways of coping with your emotions, like confiding in a trusted friend or engaging in a creative project. These activities will help you manage your emotions in a positive way. Remember, it's okay to feel your feelings and express them, but it's essential to do so in a safe and constructive way.

It's important to stay busy to keep your mind engaged and active with anything at all. When you have too much idle time, you may be overthinking or ruminating on negative thoughts. By staying busy with activities that interest you, you can keep your mind focused and prevent it from going blank. It's also a great way to boost your mood and overall well-being. However, finding a balance and not overworking yourself is crucial, as this can lead to burnout and stress. Take breaks and engage in personal activities outside the house to maintain a healthy balance.

Cognitive Distortions

Cognitive distortions refer to the biased and irrational thinking patterns that people often hold. These thinking patterns can lead to negative emotions, self-doubt, and anxiety. Examples of common cognitive distortions include all-or-nothing thinking and jumping to conclusions. When dealing with food issues, one must be aware of cognitive distortions and rigid thinking patterns that may arise. For example, you may have an all-or-nothing mentality and believe you must eat ideally. This kind of thinking can lead to extreme dieting and disordered eating habits.

Additionally, you may experience negative self-talk and think you're a failure if you eat something not on your "approved" list. Challenging and replacing these thoughts with more balanced and flexible thinking is essential. Remember that food is not the enemy; a healthy relationship involves moderation and variety of the foods you consume.

High Achievement Orientation

Many adolescents who demonstrate perfectionistic behavior hold themselves to higher standards, whether imposed by their family or themselves. They may feel immense pressure to excel academically, athletically, or socially, which puts them at a higher risk of developing control issues. The desire for perfection often leads to severe anxiety when they cannot meet their lofty expectations, resulting in disordered behavior or eating routines such as bingeing and purging to fix their perceived mistakes.

Chapter Ten

Environmental Factors

While internal factors such as psychological and genetic influences play a significant role, environmental factors also contribute to the development and progression of eating disorders. Environmental factors encompass the social, cultural, and interpersonal influences that surround individuals and can significantly impact their behaviors related to food, body image, attitudes, beliefs, and weight.

Understanding environmental factors is crucial in addressing issues related to body dissatisfaction among teenagers. By identifying and analyzing the environmental factors that contribute to this problem, we can take proactive measures that can help prevent, intervene early, and treat the issue more effectively. The environment in which teenagers live, grow, and interact plays a significant role in shaping their perceptions of beauty, body ideals, and social norms. These factors have a deep impact on the development of body dissatisfaction. Therefore, it's essential to focus on some of the critical environmental factors that have been found to contribute to this issue.

Media

Online images contribute to our body dissatisfaction, disordered eating behaviors, and poor self-esteem. The media's pervasive depictions of thinness and its ideal standard of beauty are highly accessible to adults and adolescents. The frequency of exposure to these thin images has been shown to increase psychological vulnerability to disordered eating behaviors. For example, teenagers who report frequent exposure to beauty and fashion magazines are more likely to practice dietary restriction or purging behaviors. In addition, teenagers who view thin models in magazines tend to be more dissatisfied with their bodies than those who view healthy body shapes.

Family Dynamics and Influences

Family dynamics can significantly influence their course. Family factors such as parental influence, family functioning, and eating patterns can contribute to poor body image and negative self-esteem, often precursors to lousy eating habits. Household dysfunction can take many forms, including unsupportive environments, communication issues, and restrictive family rules. A lack of emotional nurturing and support can also contribute to a dysfunctional household.

Children from families with poor communication styles, low levels of parental monitoring, and ineffective problem-solving strategies tend to develop severe symptoms. A negative self-image is greatly influenced by family life. When children are exposed to frequent criticism from their parents or inconsistent treatment from caregivers, they tend to develop low self-esteem, body dissatisfaction, and heightened vulnerability to the world around them.

Living in a hostile household environment can significantly impact an individual's mental and physical health. One of the effects of such an environment is an increase in snacking and weight gain. Adverse family conditions are characterized by high stress, tension, and conflict levels. They can result from various factors, including financial difficulties, relationship problems, and family dysfunction.

When individuals experience such stressors, they are more likely to turn to anything as a coping mechanism. Snacking in response to stress is a common way of dealing with negative emotions. Eating can provide temporary relief and comfort when feeling anxious, sad, or angry. However, this behavior can quickly become a habit, leading to gaining weight over time.

Moreover, the foods typically consumed as snacks in such situations are often high in sugar, fat, and calories. These foods provide quick energy but are also associated with a risk of obesity, heart disease, and other health problems. Negativity in the household can lead to a loss of motivation in healthy behaviors such as exercise. When constantly exposed to stress and tension, individuals may feel too drained or overwhelmed to engage in physical activity.

To address this issue, identify the underlying causes of negativity in the household and work towards resolving them. This may involve seeking counseling or therapy, improving communication among family members, or finding ways to reduce financial stressors. At the same time, individuals can take steps to manage their stress and emotions in healthier ways. If the issue is the parents, ignoring communication won't get anyone anywhere. Nothing gets fixed by going to your room and shutting the door.

Peer Influence

Spending excessive time with friends outside of school may expose adolescents to more problems and drama. Constantly listening to negativity won't help elevate one's mentality. It's essential to surround oneself with positive people who encourage personal development. Males and females are often subjected to societal pressure to conform to an ideal image of masculinity or femininity.

This image is characterized by a lean, muscular physique, and it can be challenging for many to achieve and maintain it. Peer pressure plays a significant role in perpetuating this idea and can negatively affect physical and mental health. For example, male teens may feel pressure to engage in weightlifting, sports, or other physical activities to build muscle mass and attain a more muscular physique. This pressure can come from friends, classmates, or social media influencers.

Peer pressure can also lead to unhealthy behaviors such as excessive dieting, steroid use, and other dangerous weight control practices. Teen males may feel pressured to take these measures to achieve the ideal image of masculinity, even if it comes at the cost of their health and well-being.

Moreover, masculinity or femininity can also perpetuate harmful stereotypes about male and female body sizes and shapes. For example, anyone who doesn't conform to this idea may be stigmatized or bullied, leading to low self-esteem, body dissatisfaction, and other mental health problems. To address this issue, promote positive body diversity and challenge harmful stereotypes. It can also involve encouraging healthy practices such as regular exercise, balanced diets, and stress management techniques.

Parents and educators can also play a critical role in helping teens navigate peer pressure. Building muscle is a complex process that involves both exercise and nutrition. To build muscle, the body needs to be in a calorie excess, signifying that it's consuming more calories than it's burning. This provides the body with the necessary energy to support muscle growth. However, it takes time for the body to build new muscle tissue, and this process can take anywhere from two to six years, depending on factors such as age, genetics, and exercise habits. Additionally, adequate rest and recovery time are crucial for muscle growth, as the body repairs and strengthens muscle fibers during rest periods.

Cultural and Ethnic Influences

The range of acceptable body sizes in each society is powerful in Western cultures. Models are often pressured to maintain an unrealistic and unattainable body size. Many models resort to extreme measures such as drastic dieting, fasting, and other dangerous weight control practices to achieve this. As a result, it is not uncommon for models to be starving on the job, leading to a range of consequences for their health and well-being.

These practices perpetuate harmful beauty standards, leading to serious health problems such as eating disorders, malnutrition, and other health conditions. Challenging these harmful practices and promoting healthy attitudes of societal pressure. For example, in some cultures, being overweight may be associated with wealth and prosperity, while being thin may be related to poverty and malnutrition. These stereotypes can lead to prejudice and disapproval of individuals who do not fit societal expectations.

The Movie Business

Movies are a powerful medium that shapes our views and perceptions of the world around us. They significantly impact the range of acceptable body sizes in a given society. The images and messages portrayed in movies can perpetuate unrealistic and harmful beauty standards, negatively affecting individuals' mental and physical health.

Movies often depict actors and actresses with slim, toned physiques, and this image has become synonymous with beauty and success. This pressure to conform to an ideal body size can have various negative consequences, including eating disorders, body dysmorphia, and low self-esteem. Young people are vulnerable to these messages and may feel the need to conform to societal expectations to fit in and be accepted.

One of the primary ways that movies impact the range of acceptable body sizes is through the portrayal of characters. Actors and actresses are often chosen based on their physical appearance, and the characters they play often reinforce harmful stereotypes about body size and shape. For example, male actors are often portrayed as ripped and toned, while female actors are expected to be sexy and fit. Moreover, movies can perpetuate harmful stereotypes about body size and shape based on race, ethnicity, and gender.

The entertainment business is highly competitive, and those working in the industry often face immense pressure to be outstanding or risk losing their jobs. This pressure can be particularly intense for actors, musicians, and other performers, who are expected to maintain a high level of talent and charisma to succeed in their careers.

To stand out in the entertainment business, performers may need extreme measures, such as undergoing drastic physical transformations, engaging in substance abuse, or sacrificing their personal lives. Moreover, the pressure to be extraordinary in the entertainment business can also perpetuate harmful, unfavorable outcomes.

It's important to prioritize talent, hard work, and creativity over unrealistic expectations and harmful stereotypes. Additionally, promoting healthy practices like regular exercise and balanced diets can benefit individuals both physically and mentally. Parents and educators can also play a vital role in helping young people navigate the messages portrayed in movies and other media formats. This can involve discussing the negative impacts of unrealistic standards, promoting a healthy body image, and encouraging young people to embrace their unique qualities and strengths. By doing so, we can create a more positive and accepting society.

Chapter Eleven

Importance of Social Activities

S ocial activities refer to engaging in various social interactions, group activities, and community involvement as part of their treatment and support plan. Activities are essential in addressing the emotional, cognitive, and behavioral aspects of everyone. They provide opportunities for social connection, support, and a sense of belonging for promoting mental well-being. Social activities are an excellent way to take the edge off and feel more comfortable in your day-to-day life.

Participating in social activities helps a person regain a sense of purpose and the confidence that comes with it. These activities help them to rediscover their interests, strengths, and talents, which in turn helps them to develop a renewed sense of self. They can help individuals build their self-esteem and boost their self-confidence. Through social interactions, one realizes they have value despite their circumstances. They understand they have unique qualities they can offer others, even if they are still figuring things out themselves.

Participating in social activities can open opportunities for teenagers to learn new skills, challenge their beliefs, and make practical changes.

Collaborating with others can help them see growth and rise above their current situation. Moreover, social activities can offer support from family members, teachers, and coaches, which is paramount for developing diversity. By building stronger bonds, they can foster a sense of belonging and confidence.

Hanging out with others is like having good therapy helping each other deal with issues related to the teenage years. Through social activities, teens can develop coping skills, constructively express their emotions, and become more resilient in handling future challenges. The positive impact of social activities is demonstrated by their improved grades and reduced involvement in risky behaviors.

Teenagers thrive when they have a safe place to work through their issues, feel supported by others in similar situations, learn new things, and develop new skills while helping them reconnect with themselves, others, and their communities.

Mental Health Activities

Social activities play an essential role in the lives of teenagers as they allow them to relax and unwind. Adolescents who spend less time watching TV and playing video games have better moods and improved mental health. This is because social activities help teenagers to engage with others, build relationships, and develop new skills. Team sports and other social activities can have a positive impact on mental health.

The competition and social interaction involved can be fun and can help relieve stress. Engaging in activities that they enjoy and are passionate about can improve their sense of purpose and identity. It can also help them to develop a better outlook on life and build resilience in the face of challenges. In contrast, excessive time spent watching TV and playing video games always has a negative impact on mental health. These activities can lead to isolation, decreased physical activity, and a lack of social interaction, which contributes to feelings of loneliness.

Participate in any of these for mental wellness:

Physical Activities

Teenagers can participate in various physical activities to improve their mental health, including biking, dancing, skating, or swimming. They can also jog to music or play games such as soccer, basketball, and baseball. Skating provides a healthy alternative for teenagers who love to compete but may not be interested in traditional sports.

Similarly, cycling improves mood and concentration while reducing stress levels. It also allows the individual to gain a sense of mastery over their environment by picking the best route through neighborhoods using maps and visual cues of traffic lights and signs that allow them to bike safely.

Social Clubs

Teenagers can create their own groups or join social clubs with one another that are related to their hobbies, such as photography, books, science, robotics club, or a social sports team. These activities help teenagers learn valuable new skills and meet new friends in a non-threatening way. They also encourage teens to be productive by allowing them to complete homework and participate in volunteer projects on the weekends.

Teens can also participate in service organizations, such as volunteering at food banks and animal shelters. Through these organizations, teenagers can make a difference in their own community by building unity and serving others while helping themselves.

Teens can also join a faith-based group. These social activities allow them to develop a strong sense of spirituality while offering them moral support and encouraging them to help others in the community by seeing God's work in action.

Sports or Competitive Sports

Participate in sports teams with your peers. This activity allows everyone to play with friends and learn new skills, such as being a team player. Develop the skills needed to face upcoming periods of life that will require self-confidence and good mental health, such as getting into college or a job.

Learning how to be a team player in childhood can positively impact a person's success in the job market as an adult. Employers often value teamwork and collaboration skills, as they are essential for success in many workplaces. By learning how to work effectively with others and communicate in a team setting from a young age, individuals can develop these skills and become more attractive to potential employers. Being a team player also involves being able to take constructive feedback. Additionally, teamwork can help individuals learn from others and gain new perspectives, leading to better problem-solving and innovation. Therefore, learning how to be a team player in childhood can positively impact an individual's personal and professional development.

Creative Activities

Teenagers can create art projects, build things out of recycled materials, or learn how to make web pages for social networking sites. Teens can attend a community art center to learn new skills in painting or drawing, pottery, or other artistic mediums. Some get educated on how to make things from wood, such as birdhouses, chairs, and collectibles.

Computer Activities

Teenagers can join computer clubs or study groups such as programming, graphics design, or video editing. They can also learn to use artificial intelligence for research and homework assignments. You could create video games and digital art to share with the world. Honestly, those six activities will pave the roads into the future.

Gardening Activities

Teenagers must learn how to plant, weed, and harvest to develop valuable skills that will help them appreciate the natural world and feel accomplished. Moreover, mastering the art of steam canning with mason jars is a proven technique that will be beneficial in the future. Sadly, many of the skills and knowledge that were once passed down from generation to generation are now at risk of being lost. This is because many kids today lack the opportunity to learn from their grandparents' survival talents.

This situation makes it all the more urgent for young people to take an interest in gardening and other traditional skills to preserve this knowledge for future generations. With the national deficit being around 30 trillion dollars, we could expect another great depression in the year 2032. Therefore, we must learn how to survive under harsh conditions and equip our-selves with the necessary skills to face such challenges. Benefits to mental wellness from social activities include.

Improves Mood: Group interactions with peers and adults help teenagers by encouraging them to express themselves, gain a sense of be-longing, learn skills that are necessary for daily life, and improve their mood.

Reduces Stress: Social activities provide a healthy outlet for stress re-lease through physical activities or competition in healthy environments that support the individual without criticizing their performance or im-posing unrealistic expectations.

Provides Self-Awareness: Depending on the type of social activity, teens can learn new things about themselves while connecting with others with similar interests. And building those friendships can last a lifetime. There's nothing like having friendly bonds in your youth and watching them grow over the years with memories.

Helps Relieve Symptoms of Depression: Group participation pro-vides opportunities for teens to build relationships with other kids or adults in addition to the positive feedback they receive during group ac-tivities. It can also promote belonging, reduce isolation, and help the teen feel needed.

Helps Teens Prepare for the Future: Assisting teenagers in setting goals and accomplishing them while collaborating with people from di-verse backgrounds is an excellent way to prepare them for the future.

Through participation in social activities, teenagers can polish their social skills and learn how to navigate social situations in high school, college, and beyond. These crucial skills will enable them to communicate and interact effectively with people from different walks of life, both in the short and long term. Nothing is better than working on your communication skills, getting things off your chest, and sharing life experiences while being proactive in new adventures.

We often get so caught up in the mundane routine of our daily lives that we forget to pause and reflect on our choices and actions. It's essential to understand that our decisions are significantly influenced by the amount of time, effort, and dedication we're willing to invest. Imagine an invisible line on the ground that separates our comfort zone from the unknown. Our comfort zone includes everything we're familiar with, while the unknown represents new experiences, fears, and all the wonderful things that life has to offer.

The question is, how do you choose to live your life? Are you ready to step out of your comfort zone and explore new possibilities, or are you content with staying within the limits of your comfort zone? It's important to remember that life is full of opportunities, but it's up to us to seize them.

What physical activity would you like to try out or participate in more often?

Can you think of a healthy social activity you'd like to join?

What are you doing with the hours you have that limits your capabilities?

Think about what you can change in your current lifestyle to be a better you.

Each person should have short and long-term goals for themselves. Please write down your goals so you can see them! Once you see it, believe it, you'll be able to head in that direction.

Chapter Twelve

Fitness and Mental Health

The connection between fitness and mental health has gained significant attention in recent years as research continues to highlight the positive impact of physical activity on mental well-being. Wellness, encompassing regular exercise, physical activity, and maintaining a healthy lifestyle, is vital in promoting positive mental health outcomes. The link between fitness and mental health extends beyond the physical benefits and encompasses various psychological, emotional, and cognitive aspects.

Understanding the relationship between fitness and mental health is essential for developing comprehensive strategies to enhance overall well-being. Physical activity has been shown to profoundly impact mental health, including reducing symptoms of anxiety, depression, and stress and improving overall mood. Engaging in regular exercise releases endorphins, which are neurotransmitters that promote feelings of happiness and well-being. These endorphins act as natural mood boosters, helping to alleviate symptoms.

Making Fitness a Priority in Your Life

Increasing physical activity is essential not only for improving mental health but also for overall fitness. While the benefits of regular exercise are well-documented, it is necessary to understand that regular physical activity is more than aerobic training routines or weight-bearing exercises. Regular physical activity involves muscles, such as weightlifting, walking, sports, dancing, and other forms of movement. Many people practice physical activity based on the idea that a fit body means a healthier body. The problem with this approach is that most people need to engage in more physical activity to reap these benefits.

Teens have unique challenges when incorporating physical activity into their daily lives. They're under a lot of pressure to excel academically, which can lead to stress and anxiety. On the other hand, teenagers are known for their high energy levels, making it essential to find ways to channel it positively. To make fitness a part of their lives, teens must learn how to harness their power and convert it into positive activities.

Find a Fitness Buddy

Fitness can be seen as a chore, especially if you're the only person in your household who is physically active. It can be even more daunting if you do not like exercising or feel ill-equipped to start. Finding a fitness buddy can go a long way toward helping your fitness routine become a part of your life. If you enjoy working out and finding like-minded people, incorporating exercise into your routine may become second nature and a function of your lifestyle.

Set Realistic Goals and Objectives

The overwhelming start to this project will likely leave many teens intimidated, discouraged, and frustrated. Keep the first step from getting to you. Instead, consider setting realistic goals and understand that reaching them does not happen overnight. A fundamental goal is an accurate picture of what you can achieve in a few months, not an entire year. Breaking your objective into smaller, more manageable goals makes it easier to digest what you are trying to accomplish.

Be Active Every Day

Many teenagers are sedentary or too busy doing schoolwork to exercise each day. Depending on your daily routine, consider how much time you spend watching television or sitting around at home, and then think about how much of that time could be used to be active rather than sitting around. You can easily incorporate exercise into your daily life by moving at every opportunity. By being proactive in your life, you'll grow into a motivated adult who is always looking for opportunities in life.

Little Rewards

If you want to reward yourself for exercising, consider little rewards such as free time in the evening to watch television or listen to your iPod. You can also set up more significant rewards for reaching specific fitness goals, such as buying new shoes or a new outfit to fit your workout attire.

Find a Physical Activity You Enjoy

The first step in leading a healthy and fit lifestyle is to find something you enjoy doing. This will make using your time effectively and efficiently easier while making the activity more meaningful and fun. If you do not like what you're doing, then there's no way that you'll be able to make this fitness project part of your life.

Accountability Schedule

Tracking your progress toward reaching fitness goals is an important aspect of achieving advancement. It is also essential for preventing setbacks or procrastination in your routine by reminding yourself of what you are trying to accomplish and how far along you are with this project. Rules for success can be as simple as logging your workouts on a calendar each day or writing down your progress in a fitness journal.

Take Advantage of all Facilities

Another way to make fitness a priority in your life is to take advantage of all the different kinds of fitness classes and facilities available in your area. It may seem easier to go to the same gym, practice the same sport, or run along the same path every time, but it is essential to remember that there are many other alternatives at most fitness centers. If you're bored with your routine, you must change and try something new.

Mix it up

Incorporating variety into your exercise is essential for encouraging continued participation. If you keep doing the same thing repeatedly, it will get boring, which will make you less likely to continue with your routine. Mixing up your routine will prevent boredom and help you avoid plateauing in your fitness level. If you always run the same route to work and have become bored, hop on a bike and try a new workout class at the gym or schedule an appointment with a personal trainer.

Be Consistent

The last step in this guide to starting an exercise program is maintaining consistency with your routine and efforts. Consistency is necessary to maintain even the best-laid-out fitness plans. Keep yourself from taking extended breaks in your training or skipping days.

Try to exercise daily, as it is easier to maintain a well-rounded and consistent schedule than it is to pick up an extra workout here or there. If you stay consistent with your activity, you will see results worth the effort. Incorporating exercise into your life can be challenging and may take weeks, months, or even years to continue, but if you embrace this lifestyle change and commit to it, you will be healthier for the rest of your life.

How Exercise Can Help with Depression

While traditional treatment approaches for teen depression often involve therapy and medication, exercise has emerged as a promising non-pharmacological intervention to alleviate depressive symptoms and improve mental health outcomes. Understanding how exercise can help teenagers with depression provides a valuable understanding of the potential benefits of physical conditioning as a complementary strategy to comprehensive treatment.

Teenage years are characterized by various physical, emotional, and social changes, making adolescents vulnerable to depression. Depression in teens can manifest as difficulty concentrating, persistent sadness, irritability, low self-esteem, changes in sleep, and loss of interest in previously enjoyed activities. Engaging in regular exercise has several positive effects on depression in teenagers.

Physical activity enhances body awareness, which can be especially beneficial for adolescents. Exercise encourages the creation of new neural pathways in the brain, showing improved cognitive functioning and self-awareness. Regular exercise increases energy levels, reduces fatigue and lethargy, and increases motivation to do other activities. As energy levels increase, teens can better participate in other activities or social situations that they may have previously avoided due to their depressive symptoms.

Exercise can help improve feelings of depression by enhancing neurotransmitters that regulate moods, such as serotonin and dopamine. These neurotransmitters serve as chemical messengers in the brain, causing various emotional and mood-related reactions such as pain, anger, and depression. When these neurotransmitters are enhanced through regular exercise, this can help alleviate symptoms of depression.

Exercise is also essential for maintaining or improving healthy weight for adolescents with depression and other conditions such as obesity and eating disorders. Achieving a healthy body weight helps adolescents feel more positive about themselves and improve their confidence. This improves their self-esteem by giving them a sense of accomplishment they may not have felt otherwise while enhancing their overall quality of life.

Physical activity helps improve academic grades and school performance by improving concentration, motivation, and academic performance. Avoid poor school performance; be an example of productivity by avoiding procrastination and laziness. A regular structured exercise program can help prevent this issue and promote healthy habits, which are important for mental health.

Regular activity reduces the risks of substance abuse by promoting healthy eating habits and increasing self-esteem. Exercise helps teens develop high levels of motivation in the classroom, which leads to more significant progress and higher academic achievement than they may have otherwise achieved.

It'll improve adolescent social relationships by promoting healthy interpersonal skills and helping teens become more socially competent with others, thereby improving the overall quality of life. This development in interpersonal skills helps build strong social bonds that support adolescents when they feel low due to depression or other mental health issues.

Exercise helps build muscles and tone physique, creating a more positive perception of one's physical attributes. This may help teens become more socially competent and feel better about their physical appearance in social situations by boosting their self-esteem. Exercises that promote concentration, such as running or other rhythmical exercises like swimming and cycling, can be especially effective in reducing anxiety.

By seeing yourself in motion, you'll believe in yourself to accomplish much more than you imagined. It's essential to push yourself to move beyond your comfort zone and challenge yourself. When you take on new challenges and see yourself progressing, you build self-confidence and a sense of accomplishment that can motivate you to take on even more significant challenges in the future. So, get up and get moving! You'll be surprised at what you can achieve when you believe in yourself.

Chapter Thirteen

Substance Abuse

Depression is not just a part of growing up. Whether it's for a few days or months, these emotions affect your ability to function in everyday life. Substance abuse can cause these unbalanced feelings, but many other explanations exist. It's concerning that approximately 3% of teens and a handful of teachers are indicated for drug sales in high school. This means that a small but significant portion of high school students are acquiring these illegal and dangerous drugs to sell to anyone looking for a good time.

Drug sales in schools can lead to numerous negative consequences, including legal action, expulsion, and even criminal charges. This leads to theft or borrowing finances and trafficking substances all over the place and even your home. Adolescents who use drugs are at a higher risk of developing addiction, mental health, and physical health problems. Moreover, drug use can negatively impact academic performance and social relationships and destroy your chances of entering college or even the armed forces.

When teens are experiencing depression, they may use drugs to cope with it. While this can seem like an easy solution at first glance, substance abuse will compound their depression or anxiety over time, making it harder to live without drugs despite wanting to and needing help more than ever.

The connection between depression and substance misuse is a tricky and significant issue affecting all individuals at any age. Substance abuse refers to the harmful use of drugs or alcohol. At the same time, depression is a mental health condition characterized by persistent sadness, hopelessness, and a loss of interest in activities. These two conditions often coexist and can profoundly impact an individual's physical, emotional, and social well-being.

Substance abuse is multifaceted, and the exact nature of the connection can vary from person to person. For some individuals, substance abuse is a way to self-medicate or cope with overwhelming emotions. They may turn to drugs or alcohol as a means of temporarily alleviating their depressive symptoms or escaping emotional pain. In other cases, substance abuse may trigger or exacerbate symptoms of depression, leading to a vicious cycle of worsening mental health.

Substance abuse and depression often go hand-in-hand because drugs and alcohol can directly impact an individual's brain chemistry. When a drug or alcohol enters the body, it can affect the levels of neurotransmitters in the brain, such as dopamine and serotonin. Dopamine is involved with feelings of pleasure, while serotonin is responsible for regulating moods, anxiety levels, and sleep patterns. These chemicals are affected by substance abuse in at least two ways.

First, substance use may serve as a way to trigger symptoms of depression that may already exist in an individual's brain chemistry. Depression also has a significant genetic component. Some people are more prone to depression than others. Substance abuse can heighten the risk of depression by altering brain chemicals, making it more likely for a person to experience depressive symptoms.

Second, substance use can cause depression directly. Over time, it will cause neurotransmitters to become imbalanced in the brain, causing a chemical imbalance similar to that of a person experiencing depression. As a result, an individual may start feeling depressed without any previous mental health symptoms or risk factors.

For many who struggle with depression, substance abuse may feel like their only means of coping. It can be difficult and disruptive to deal with a mental health condition without the proper help. Young adults who are suicidal or depressed may have difficulty accessing mental health care for various reasons, such as cost, stigmatization, inadequate insurance coverage, and even misinformation.

Without proper treatment for depression and other mental health conditions, the likelihood of recovery and the time it takes to do so increases. Nonprescription drugs and depression don't mix; seeking treatment as soon as possible is essential for several reasons.

Substance abuse is not the only reason someone may experience depression. It may help to identify other stressors in a person's life that might contribute to their feelings of sadness or hopelessness. For example, depression or anxiety may result from financial difficulties, interpersonal conflicts, or other problems. A teen might know world issues like poverty, hunger, violence, and injustice. They may feel helpless to make a change in the world they live in.

A teen might be surrounded by others who are depressed or facing addiction, increasing the chances of feeling alone or in pain. There might be unrealistic expectations of themselves; perhaps the goals were too high. Or there's a disappointment of not achieving anything, leading them to frustration. Some of the biggest reasons teens have moved to drugs are they don't value themselves and feel stupid, unattractive, and, in some cases, unlovable.

In the event of many earthly temptations, they may give in to sinful desires to cope with their pain. Substance abuse feels like it's providing some relief at the moment but worsens and prolongs depressive symptoms in the long term. Teens and young adults may be reluctant to seek treatment for depression. Some may be embarrassed by their feelings of sadness and are afraid that telling others will make them appear weak or unable to function in school or work.

Some may fear that they have nothing to offer besides chemical relief, which is often not the case; therefore, substance abuse can be a symptom of depression rather than the cause. Depression is often complicated, and it can be challenging to identify all the contributing factors. It's common for young adults struggling with depression to have experienced trauma, such as abuse or neglect, in the home.

A drug or alcohol addiction can make an individual more vulnerable to depression because it impairs their ability to think clearly or make decisions. It also increases vulnerability to stress and conflicts at home, which leads to a means of escape or coping. Individuals are more likely to experience side effects from those substances, such as nausea and drug cravings.

Although it may feel like a quick fix, it can increase feelings of depression over time through its continued use and cause various emotional side effects. An individual struggling with drugs and alcohol is more likely to suffer from addiction and become dependent on substances to manage their symptoms of depression.

Managing Peer Pressure

Adolescents often face peer pressure, which can have a significant impact on their substance use. It refers to the influence of peers, especially friends, to conform to specific behaviors that are deemed socially acceptable. When confronted with difficult choices, teens usually seek support or approval from their peers. And if friends are involved in substance abuse, such as alcohol or drugs, it can be a risky combination that may lead you down the same path. Remember, you become who you associate with, so pay attention and consider finding a new group of friends if necessary.

How can teens manage peer pressure and substance abuse?

Choose Friends Wisely

As teens mature, they desire their peers' acceptance more than adults' acceptance. They need to make good choices regarding who they befriend. Some friends may negatively influence and lead you down a dangerous path. Support groups and mentoring programs are excellent ways for teens to make good friendships, but it is essential to choose these wisely. Teens in these groups should be positive, respectable, skilled role models.

Get Involved in Positive Organizations

Join clubs and groups that are positive and engaging. Socializing with others is critical for teens to form healthy friendships, so it is important not to lock your child in the house. Getting involved in sports teams, scouting groups, or other activities that will bring them into contact with other people is a great way to meet like-minded peers who can help prevent teens from straying down the wrong path.

Establish Healthy Rules

Teens need clear guidelines about when and where alcohol and drugs are allowed. This promotes a sense of responsibility and respect for their health and the safety of others. There are age restrictions on alcohol, and there's a huge difference between legal and illegal drugs and directions to follow when prescribed. It's also important to establish consequences for breaking the rules.

Educate Themselves about the Risks

Teens should be given the facts about the risks of alcohol and drug abuse. They should be aware of the short and long-term effects that could affect their ability to succeed in school or relationships. Identifying these problems early in life is essential for teens to develop healthy self-esteem that does not rely on others' approval.

Seek Support from Trusted Adults

Teens need to seek support from adults who can provide perspective about the problems that both individuals and teens face. Having a mentor to turn to in times of distress can help the teen avoid falling into a pattern of substance abuse.

Set an Example

This is not only a good idea, but it's also essential for teens to know that their parents are setting an excellent example for them. Good role models are crucial, so parents need to practice what they preach. Parents should be careful about how much alcohol and drugs they consume in front of their children and what language they use when referring to these substances.

Engage in Positive Activities and Hobbies

An excellent way for teens to avoid the pitfalls of substance abuse is to focus all their time and energy on positive activities. They should get involved in clubs, sports, and other things that will positively occupy them. Having something else that is fulfilling will help them feel like they do not need outside influences like alcohol and drugs.

Practice Assertiveness and Refusal Skills

Teenagers are developing skill sets that can help them navigate through difficult times. Teens need to learn how to be assertive and refuse drugs and alcohol. Setting boundaries or limits will help them avoid falling into a pattern of substance abuse. If people say, "Everyone's doing it," they are certainly not. Don't fall to the broken world.

Admit Feelings

Teens must practice telling others how they feel, even if saying it might make them uncomfortable or look weak. The more readily they express their emotions, the less likely they will turn to alcohol or drugs because being honest has been found to lead to better relationships with others. If you're unhappy with your choices, take action for yourself. This is one of the most important steps to improving your life. Remain vigilant and committed to staying on track. Ultimately, you'll have a better chance of succeeding if you're caring for yourself versus waiting until things worsen.

Follow Through Each Day

No matter how difficult a day may be, make sure each day ends positively by looking back and evaluating what went well and what did not. This will help you decide how to approach the next day. Substance abuse can be a complex problem to overcome on any level, but teens who can avoid it do much better than those who fall into a pattern of use or abuse. Parents must monitor and oversee their teen's interactions. This can be done through discussions, monitoring their activities, and setting clear limits on when and where the substances are allowed. These strategies can help prevent substance abuse, whether alcohol, marijuana, or other drugs.

Energy Drinks

Not everything is about illegal drugs; other active stimulants complicate the mind. Energy drinks have increasingly become popular, especially among young adults. While these drinks may provide a quick energy boost, they can also cause crashes and other adverse effects on health. The primary issue with energy drinks is their high caffeine content.

Many energy drinks contain caffeine levels that are much higher than those found in coffee or soda. This leads to a sudden surge of energy, followed by a crash when the caffeine wears off. This can result in feelings of difficulty concentrating, irritability, and fatigue.

Moreover, energy drinks often contain high levels of artificial sugar, contributing to weight gain and heart problems. Excessive intake leaves the individual feeling even more tired and sluggish. In addition to caffeine, other stimulants, such as taurine and guarana, are found inside these beverages. These substances can further aggravate the adverse effects of caffeine and contribute to crashes and other health issues.

Watch an adult who drinks coffee each day. Take the coffee away, and you'll see a grumpy, upset, over-the-top, losing their mind, can't function, all because they didn't have these store-bought drugs. Overall, you want to be watchful of what you put in your body; all forms of legal or illegal drugs mess with your mind and behaviors.

Chapter Fourteen

Seeking Professional Help

Depression affects the well-being of relationships, academic performance, and overall quality of life. While self-help strategies and support from friends and family can be beneficial, the expertise and guidance of mental health professionals are often needed to provide comprehensive and effective care.

Professional help for teens with depression typically involves engaging with mental health professionals, such as psychologists, psychiatrists, therapists, or counselors who specialize in working with adolescents. These professionals possess the knowledge, experience, and therapeutic techniques to meet the unique needs and concerns of teenagers experiencing rough times. Seeking professional help offers several benefits, such as:

Accurate diagnosis and assessment: Mental health professionals are trained to conduct thorough evaluations and diagnose depression. They can differentiate between depression and other mental health conditions, assess the severity of symptoms, and identify any co-occurring underlying factors contributing to depression. An accurate diagnosis lays the foundation for appropriate treatment planning.

Customized treatment plans: Health professionals work collaboratively with teens and their families to develop personalized treatment plans custom-tailored to their needs and circumstances. These plans may involve various therapeutic modalities, such as cognitive-behavioral therapy, dialectical behavior therapy, interpersonal therapy, or medication if deemed necessary. Professional help ensures that interventions are evidence-based, targeted, and comprehensive.

Emotional support and validation: Adolescence can be an emotionally challenging period, and teens with depression often feel misunderstood or invalidated by others. Mental health professionals provide a safe, non-judgmental space for teens to express their thoughts, emotions, and concerns. They offer empathetic support, validate their experiences, and help teens navigate the complexities of their feelings, fostering a sense of understanding and emotional well-being.

Learning coping strategies and life skills: Professional help equips teenagers with essential coping strategies and life skills to manage their depression effectively. Mental health professionals teach practical tools for recognizing and challenging negative thought patterns, regulating emotions, improving communication, building resilience, and problem-solving. These skills empower teens to navigate the challenges of depression and develop a strong foundation for long-term well-being.

Monitoring progress and preventing relapse: Regular sessions with mental health professionals allow for ongoing monitoring of a teen's progress and the effectiveness of their treatment plan. Professionals can identify signs of relapse, adjust interventions as needed, and provide continuous support throughout recovery.

It's essential to encourage and support teens in seeking professional help for depression. Parents, educators, and healthcare providers play a crucial role in recognizing the signs of depression, initiating conversations, and facilitating access to appropriate professional resources. By addressing depression with professional guidance, teens can enhance their well-being, develop effective coping mechanisms, and improve their overall quality of life.

When to Seek Expert Advice

Seeking expert advice is often essential in treating and recovering a teenager suffering from depression. Adolescence is a period of significant emotional and physical changes, and it's not uncommon for teens to experience ups and downs in their moods. However, when symptoms of depression persist, interfere with daily functioning, and significantly impact a teenager's overall quality of life, it becomes crucial to seek professional guidance.

Knowing when to seek expert advice can be challenging, as every individual's experience with depression is unique. Seeking expert advice is recommended when a teenager consistently experiences overwhelming sadness, emptiness, hopelessness, or despair that lasts for more than two weeks. It may indicate clinical depression. These emotions may interfere with their daily functioning, relationships, and well-being.

Teens could experience persistent symptoms of low energy, fatigue, or psychomotor impairment. They may feel tired and unmotivated, have difficulty concentrating, and have poor impulse control. These symptoms often interfere with their ability to perform daily tasks, socialize with peers, and participate in extracurricular activities. When personal performance declines, watch out for starting and stopping tasks, slowed speech, and reduced cognitive function.

They could experience persistent sleep problems, including difficulty falling asleep, restless sleep, early morning awakenings, and waking up during the night. These significantly interfere with their ability to function throughout the day, and they experience significant struggles to fall asleep at night. Many teens face the possibility of transient insomnia.

When a teenager exhibits signs of hopelessness, worthlessness, thoughts of suicide or self-harm, or attempts to take their own life, it's paramount to seek emergency help to prevent further harm. Teenagers who abuse alcohol, prescription medications, and illicit drugs and engage in self-harming behaviors like cutting themselves may have underlying mental health conditions requiring additional assistance.

Teenagers with clinical depression may experience losing their temper and may have frequent conflicts with family members, peers, or friends. This hostility towards others occasionally leads to thoughts of suicidal actions. It's vital to seek expert advice as soon as possible.

Teenagers with clinical depression often experience regular signs of aggression and reckless behavior. They have frequent fights at school and difficulties managing anger, irritability, and moodiness. This aggressive behavior may occasionally lead to physical altercations, resulting in injuries.

Aggressive behavior may also impact a teenager's relationships with family members, friends, coaches, teachers, or other students. These attitudes significantly interfere with their ability to function and maintain healthy relationships with peers and family members within the school community.

Mental health professionals, such as psychologists, youth ministers, therapists, or psychiatrists, have the expertise to assess, diagnose, and develop appropriate treatment plans for teen depression. Parents, teachers, and other trusted adults can provide support by facilitating conversations, offering encouragement, and helping access professional resources. Early intervention and professional guidance are vital for improving outcomes and assisting teenagers to effectively manage and recover from depression.

Clinical depression goes beyond the typical mood fluctuations that most people experience and significantly affects their thoughts, emotions, behaviors, and overall well-being. The symptoms experienced by teens with depression can interfere with having a healthy life and maintaining relationships with peers and family members within the school community.

The good news is that depression can be handled effectively. With the right treatment plan, clinicians can help teenagers attain positive mental health outcomes. Clinical depression can be effectively treated with psychotherapy and medication.

Psychotherapy

Psychotherapy is a highly effective treatment strategy. It provides an opportunity for teenagers with clinical depression to explore what has happened in their lives, identify negative thought patterns, and develop new skills and attitudes to manage the symptoms of depression. Effective psychotherapy programs will help teenagers develop positive coping skills and ways to handle stressful situations that may trigger depressive symptoms.

It also allows adolescents to gain insight into their feelings, connect with others positively, and develop healthy ways of dealing with conflict. Therapists can help teenagers understand why they feel the way they do, think about how their behavior affects others, and learn new ways to cope with these feelings.

Psychological counseling is also available at no cost through many communities' mental health centers. Teens and their families can seek out more intensive treatment options from psychiatrists. Several medications can treat clinical depression safely and effectively. These medications allow teenagers to experience fewer physical symptoms and fewer depressive thoughts. They also allow teenagers to function more effectively in all areas of life.

The most common medications used to treat depression in adolescents are antidepressant drugs, such as selective serotonin reuptake inhibitors. Prozac and Paxil work by helping brain cells release more serotonin than they would otherwise, an essential mood-regulating substance. These medications can temporarily improve depressive symptoms and are considered safer than antidepressant medication, but may also cause several serious side effects. Therefore, talk with your doctor about the benefits and risks of the treatment options.

Combining psychotherapy with antidepressant medication is the most effective method for treating clinical depression in teenagers. The combination of medication and psychotherapy has been shown to offer significant benefits over antidepressant medication alone. A critical aspect of effective treatment for depression in teenagers is developing new skills and attitudes to deal with daily situations, such as peer relationships, school, and anything happening with a part-time job.

Treatment planners will work with teenagers and their families to develop new skills to help each person accomplish their daily goals. It's just as important for teenagers with clinical depression to access community support systems, school support, and family involvement. Educating family members about the nature of depression is essential in establishing appropriate support and care. Parents should create more open lines of communication within the home, understand what their child may be going through, and reduce any anger or frustration during this process.

Clinical depression is a severe and potentially harmful condition in teenagers. There is no single cause of depression. Instead, many different factors may put a teenager at risk for developing clinical depression. For instance, family history, social support, school environment, stressors in society, genetics, and sexuality are all elements that can contribute to the beginning of clinical depression in teenagers.

The Fundamentals

Each needs to know they can seek help without feeling helpless or ashamed. There is a light at the end of this impossibly dark tunnel, though it may seem out of reach. People who suffer from depression and anxiety are not just "crazy" or "weird." They can have real, diagnosable conditions that can be treated with medication, therapy, or both. Anxiety is no different from any other chronic condition in the way that it should be recognized as needing treatment.

Our medical community has not recognized the link between cognitive and physical health. Often, when talking about anxiety and depression, we treat it like a "disorder" instead of a condition. Anxiety and depression are well-recognized psychological disruptions experienced by millions of people in our country. The problem is most people who suffer from these disturbances do not see them as needing medical intervention. Nearly 12% of adults experience anxiety. Many more experience milder forms of anxiety but feel it's silly or embarrassing to talk about their feelings.

The stigma surrounding anxiety and depression is slowly fading, and more people are coming forward to tell their stories and seek help. Many of them do so because they're tired of suffering in silence. The first step to recovery from anxiety or depression is to educate yourself about how it affects your life. It can be challenging to admit you have a problem. The good news is that incredible remedies are available once you recognize you're trying to cope with anxiety.

It's a lot easier than you think to take care of yourself. People who suffer from anxiety and depression often go through the motions of their daily lives, but they're not truly living because they don't know what happiness or joy feels like. They don't know what it's like to be free of their daily heavyweight. But they can find out and feel what it's like to live life to the fullest.

Sufferers may think there is no life beyond their situation, but there is. Many people who suffer from depression are now leading happy, fulfilling lives. And it's important to remember that it takes courage and strength to do so, but any good thing in life requires hard work. One of the most difficult things about overcoming anxiety or depression is challenging old thoughts and behaviors.

Teens aren't lacking in intelligence or willpower; they are fighting themselves. There is nothing shameful about being afraid, sad, exhausted, or suffering in any way. Dispel the myths about anxiety and depression that you've grown up believing and begin on your path to a happier, healthier life. A diagnosis of anxiety disorder isn't the end of the world. It's a difficult journey, but there are ways to get better.

Chapter Fifteen

Risks of Medication

Prescriptions for teen depression, such as antidepressants, have benefits and possible side effects that must be carefully considered. Prescribed antidepressant medications by health professionals to help alleviate their symptoms and improve their mental state. These medications target neurotransmitters in the brain, such as serotonin, to regulate mood and emotions. They can be beneficial in reducing symptoms of depression and restoring a teenager's ability to function.

However, it's essential to recognize that medication is not a one-size-fits-all solution. For instance, some teenagers may experience side effects ranging from mild to severe headaches, weight gain, sleep disturbances, or even increased feelings of restlessness or suicidal thoughts.

Dangers of Antidepressants in Teens

While these medications can effectively alleviate symptoms, it's paramount to be aware of the issues associated with their use. The use of antidepressants in this age bracket requires careful consideration and monitoring due to various factors impacting safety and effectiveness. Antidepressants help teenagers regain emotional balance and engage in daily life. However, it's necessary to recognize that antidepressants have these risks and side effects that must be thoroughly understood. These include:

Severe Reactions

Antidepressants are designed to alter the activity of neurotransmitters in the brain. While this helps to alleviate depressive symptoms, it can also intensify them in some cases. In rare instances, an antidepressant can cause a severe reaction that leads to serious conditions. The chances of having a severe reaction are increased if the medication is taken in higher doses than your doctor recommends or if taken with other drugs that affect your central nervous system. These include alcohol, illicit drugs, and certain cold medications.

Risk of Addiction

A significant concern of antidepressant use is potentially developing a substance abuse disorder. While drugs like cocaine and alcohol are commonly associated with addiction and substance abuse in adults, antidepressants can lead to the same adverse consequences. Antidepressant use has been linked to developing conditions that can be hard to manage if left untreated.

Suicidal Thoughts or Actions

Some suicidal thoughts and behaviors have been reported in people taking antidepressants with no history or risk factors for suicide attempts. The FDA still approved these prescriptions for use and issued several warnings and recommendations regarding using antidepressant medications in teenagers. Any concerns about medication or side effects should be discussed directly with a doctor or therapist.

Long-Term Effects

One of the biggest concerns with antidepressant use in teenagers is their long-term impact on the developing brain. Antidepressants are known to have neurotoxic effects, even though they are not considered hazardous and don't cause long-term damage. Recognize that these medications can affect the brain in other ways and lead to complications, such as the risk of depression or anxiety, feeling numb, carelessness of other people, reduced feelings, weight gain, and in adulthood, different types of sexual problems.

For the sake of the reading audience, those adult sexual specifics will not be listed in this book. Discuss your concerns and questions directly with your doctor if any concerning situation arises.

Changes in Mood

Antidepressants can be highly effective, helping teenagers return to their normal emotional state and engage in daily activities. However, some teens may experience changes that are different than expected, especially when starting a new treatment plan. Mood changes can include persistent sadness or despair, experiencing sudden bursts of anger or aggression, unusual irritability during the day, and more. In some cases, the symptoms of depression may worsen during medication use.

Restlessness and Fatigue

Anytime you're using antidepressants, you could feel restless and tired daily as part of the medication treatment plan. Some experiences may be more intense than others, but it's essential to recognize the possible changes to your physical state. The restlessness and fatigue typically associated with antidepressant use can make it difficult for teenagers to focus on any given activity. It may also be symptomatic of underlying chemical imbalances and worsening depression.

Changes in Weight and Appetite

Antidepressants may cause weight changes in teens, resulting in difficulties managing weight and obesity. Some teenagers may experience an increase in appetite, while others might experience a reduction. Changes in appetite can influence your ability to maintain a healthy diet and exercise routine.

Changes in Concentration and Ability to Focus

Teenagers who are using antidepressants may have a difficult time concentrating on tasks, remembering things, or completing their schoolwork. They may also struggle to focus on any given subject or event. Changes in concentration can make it difficult for a teenager to engage in meaningful conversations with friends and family members, leading to isolation and withdrawal from their loved ones.

Changes in Sleep

Odd symptoms emerge during medication use, such as a sudden increase or decrease in sleep. This could indicate the medicine is working by calming them down, or they became worse than they were before. Suppose your teenager is experiencing these symptoms repeatedly. In that case, speak to their doctor to determine if they are experiencing an adverse drug effect or other underlying medical conditions. You may notice changes in sleep patterns over time. You may need to examine your teenager's bedroom more closely to determine if there is anything unusual about their sleeping environment.

Slowed Growth and Development

The use of antidepressants in teens has been linked to various physical, emotional, and mental complications that vary in severity depending on each specific medication. Antidepressants are associated with a degree of risk for slow growth, which can be particularly concerning for teenagers still growing and developing. The rate of change can be influenced by various factors related to the medications, such as dosage, frequency, and duration of use.

Decreased Personal Interests

Teenagers using antidepressants may experience a decrease or a complete loss of interest in their relationships. Some emotions or attractions could be limited as the mind is being altered. Watch for a reduction in expressing heartfelt moments or emotional pain as motivation is lost.

Unexplained Behavioral Changes

Significant behavior changes, such as increased aggression, impulsivity, or reckless conduct, may be warning signs of adverse reactions to antidepressants. Pay attention to sudden shifts in personality, unusual risk-taking, or problematic behavior that seems out of character for the teenager. If your teenager is prone to mood swings and erratic behavior, you should be incredibly attentive to any changes that occur while they are using antidepressants.

It's common for teenagers who are taking antidepressant medications to experience mood swings that are pretty similar to symptoms of depression but are not as severe. In some cases, this can complicate the adolescent's treatment plan, requiring a change in medication or additional therapy sessions to resolve them effectively.

Seizures

Antidepressants can potentially cause seizures in some cases due to their ability to influence neurotransmitter activity in the brain. While these seizures are not common, they can lead to serious medical complications and pose significant risks when they occur.

Skin Reactions

Allergic skin reactions, such as a rash or hives, can occur in some people and may be triggered by certain antidepressants. Such symptoms are often mild and do not pose a significant risk to most people. However, those with allergies or other preexisting medical conditions may have a more severe reaction that warrants medical attention.

Dizziness

Antidepressants have the potential to cause dizziness and drowsiness, particularly when they first begin to take effect and during dosage adjustments. These side effects can make it difficult for teens to concentrate in school or other settings. They can also increase the chances of motor vehicle accidents due to slowed reaction times, fatigue, and poor coordination.

Nausea

Some antidepressant medications cause nausea, particularly when taken on an empty stomach or combined with certain foods or drinks. While nausea is not associated with significant health risks, it can be uncomfortable and lead to poor appetite control or malnutrition if it persists. If the teenager is having trouble keeping food down due to these medications. In that case, you should speak to their doctor to see if switching medications or adjusting the dosage schedule can resolve this issue.

Headache and Fatigue

Severe fatigue and a persistent headache can indicate an adverse drug reaction. Suppose these symptoms are associated with the use of antidepressants. In that case, your teenager must contact their doctor to pinpoint the trigger and determine how to avoid this risk.

Bruising and bleeding can occasionally occur when antidepressants are taken; it can cause inflammation and increase the chances of bleeding. They can be particularly troublesome if they persist or are associated with a significant fall in blood pressure. If your teenager is experiencing these symptoms, they must take a comprehensive medical examination to examine the cause.

Respiratory Distress

Antidepressants can induce distress in teenagers prone to panic attacks or have an underlying condition that affects their breathing. These side effects may make it difficult for them to breathe deeply enough for adequate oxygen intake, which can result in exhaustion and respiratory distress in some cases.

Increased Pressure in the Eyes

There could be an increase in pressure inside the eye, causing a condition called glaucoma. It can be particularly concerning for teenagers prone to developing eye diseases if this occurs. Suppose your teenager is experiencing severe and unusual eye pain accompanied by ringing or a full sensation in the ear lasting longer than usual. In that case, they must see a doctor as soon as possible to determine if another condition, such as an infection or vision issue, might be at play.

These are just a few examples of possible side effects that a teen may experience due to antidepressant medication use. Not all warning signs indicate an adverse reaction to antidepressants, but it's better to be cautious and proactive in addressing concerns. Healthcare professionals can assess the situation and determine the appropriate course of action.

Discontinuation and Withdrawal Effects

Antidepressants can profoundly impact the brain, especially when they are abruptly discontinued or stopped after long-term treatment. During the process of discontinuation, you may experience withdrawal symptoms that include feelings of nausea, headaches, and dizziness. While these symptoms can be uncomfortable, they are generally not considered dangerous. Symptoms could take one month per year spent on the medication. However, some people may experience more severe complications if they quit cold turkey versus slowly cycling off.

Chapter Sixteen

Bad Acquaintances

The power of environment and relationships can be taken as a place importance on your surroundings. It can be a reminder that their environment is not suitable for them anymore. It's hard to argue against this notion because depression often stems from significant problems in your life, such as abuse or addiction and bad acquaintances. However, it's essential to note that you cannot completely separate the power of environment and relationships from the power of mental health.

We cannot completely escape the fact that our environment and relationships will have some influence on our mental health because it's complex to measure and communicate. But we can take comfort in knowing we can take steps to change who we choose to be around without changing who we are as a person. Teens and adults should not be limited by living in a particular place or with certain people. They can change who they're around without trying to change themselves.

Removing Oneself from Toxic Individuals

Toxic individuals come from all ages with different mindsets. Whether it's an abusive person online or someone who crosses your path, poisonous people can sustain depression, creating a lingering effect. These knuckle-heads enjoy cranking up nonsense on someone else. It's just another person you have to ignore or click the block button. Having a toxic friend or family member correlates with the assertive after-effects in our environments.

These friends or family members can lead you into dark and unhealthy places without your knowledge or consent. They can pull you into depression and increase your pain when you only want to be happy and healthy. They have no regard for your mental health and intentionally willingly drag you through misery if that's what they desire. Some examples would be mental trickery, guilt trips, using years of wisdom against you, discussion by comparison, and going after your weaknesses. While it hurts, one can only be in a toxic environment for so long. Eventually, we will learn how to take a turn for the better in our reality. How can teens remove themselves from Toxic individuals?

Let Go of the Toxic Person

This is the most challenging step. We cannot allow people to hurt us. Understand that these people were once our friends, either by a relationship or you've met them through life's pursuits. It's essential to let go of these toxic people because they are no good for you. They will only cause more harm than good if you continue in their presence.

You might endure pain and be met with a ton of resistance; it's best to separate yourself from these destructive people. We will always have toxic people in our lives. It's impossible to get rid of them all. But we must learn how to deal with them to avoid unnecessary damage that could have long-term effects.

Accept the Fact That You Cannot Change Someone

Many believe you can change individuals into better people; the truth is that you cannot change anyone else, only yourself. Everyone is different and can only change themselves; accepting this will allow you to push forward and respect yourself because it's no longer based on someone else's opinion.

Look for Others to Replace the Negativity

It's best to find a way to eliminate and replace these toxic people from your life and replace them with others who keep you going strong. No one can tell you exactly where to find these people; search and discover new friends who are willing to accept you for who you are. You will become successful when you have others positively influencing your life.

This will take time; do your part in helping them, and they, in turn, can become the people who will impact your life. We cannot control anyone else, but we can control ourselves. We must be able to adapt when necessary to change the outcome of our lives.

Set Boundaries

When you're around toxic people, you must set boundaries with them. You cannot let them treat you negatively; you have the right to defend yourself. We must be able to protect ourselves from anyone who wishes to harm us. This does not mean striking back physically, but it does mean being firm with our words and making it known that we will not put up with anything less than what we deserve from these people.

They will no longer be allowed to control your emotions and thereby lose the power they think they have over you. You can tell them nobody will make fun of you, hurt you, or get the better of you.

Build a Supportive Network

Though many still live in toxic environments, building a network of supportive individuals is essential. It would be best to find people you can count on. To help you in any situation. Be available when needed, as those qualities are in a great friend. This will enable you to have a network of people who support you, especially when things get tough. Remember that it's not always about the situation. Sometimes, it takes one person to tell us how important we are, and we'll find our place in the world.

We must learn to embrace these people without feeling sad or hurt because this releases chemicals in our brains that can cause even more harm if we're not paying attention. We must be willing to rely on others when we have no one else to turn to. If we can get past this, the road ahead will be much easier by replacing emotional burdens with happier moments.

Focus on Personal Growth

It's essential to focus on personal growth to move past our situations. The more we focus on ourselves, the faster we can pick ourselves up when the going gets tough. We must continue to build up positive qualities about ourselves rather than focusing solely on the negatives in our lives.

Once you have developed yourself positively, you'll see that nothing can hold you back. Focus on things you can control, not on anything outside your reach. Never forget to make a plan of action for yourself and then stick with it no matter what. When you set a goal, it reduces the chances of failure. See it, feel it, become your destiny. Removing yourself from toxic individuals may not be easy or immediate. Be patient with yourself and allow for gradual changes. Surround yourself with positivity and prioritize your mental health. With time and the proper support, you can distance yourself from toxic individuals and create a healthier, more supportive environment that contributes to your overall well-being.

Mental Sanity

Understanding the role of the people around you determines a person's mental state and how you'll feel at any point. The place you reside and the company you keep are among other factors that determine your way of life, shaping your thoughts and expectations. Your environment is significant to your mental health because it defines how you live. For instance, if you reside in a community with harmful and toxic people, your chances of becoming unhappy are higher than if you placed yourself with positive people.

You can relate to others to improve your perspective on different issues. You should move from a bad environment and start living in a new one with supportive people who don't encourage negativity. This will allow you to embrace positivity and enlighten your thought processes, changing how you approach different issues. How you choose to live determines the people you associate with. If you surround yourself in an environment where corruption, drug use, and immorality are widespread, then chances are you will get involved with such activities and engage in immoral behavior. On the other hand, if you live in a place with lots of positive activities to engage in, you'll most certainly get involved. This leads to individuals living in that environment being of sound mind and spirit, which indicates a healthy mental state.

Your environment largely determines how you relate to others. For instance, if the people you associate with have a positive outlook toward life, this will rub off on you and make you more productive. Just like the opposite, if you associate with people who are narrow-minded and negative about different things, chances are you'll become like them due to their proximity.

Negative people are generally more narrow-minded than those with a positive outlook. Therefore, if you want to take charge of your environment and make it conducive to living a happy, healthy, and productive life, you may need to reconsider how you use your time, money, and relaxation moments. Discover new places where people are supportive and broad-minded. This way, you transition your life in the direction you desire. Always concentrate on your studies and avoid being exposed to negativity that may adversely affect your lifestyle choices.

Prioritize your mental health as it forms the foundation of your life. Our mindset shapes how we perceive the world and respond to various situations. Therefore, it's essential to cultivate a conducive environment that promotes our well-being and happiness. It affects our relationships with others and enables us to attain our ambitions more efficiently.

Chapter Seventeen

Understanding People

S uccessful social interactions necessitate a good grasp of people and relationships. It allows you to make informed decisions about interacting with others based on their motivations and behaviors. However, teenagers often struggle with this because they lack life experience and are learning through trial and error. Navigating social relationships can be incredibly challenging. You need to understand the dynamics of real people, fake people, and alternative impression fake people to protect your mental well-being and establish authentic connections.

Real people genuinely care about your well-being and provide support through the ups and downs of life. They offer empathy, understanding, and nonjudgmental support and build relationships founded on honesty, trust, and mutual respect. Having real people in your life can provide a strong support network that benefits your mental health. At the same time, honest people can be level-headed with you by disagreeing with your thoughts and actions as they exchange their opinions. Real people can be friendly without being condescending or suspicious and can offer sound advice without being bossy or jealous.

On the other hand, recognizing fake people is paramount. They may exhibit signs of poor chemistry or lie about their intentions, making it difficult to distinguish them from genuine people. Fake people may exploit your vulnerabilities for their own benefit. Fake people pose as friends but only care about fulfilling their personal needs. They offer insincere support and friendship that suits them and are quick to criticize, gossip, and mistreat you when you're not around. These relationships are built on deception and exploitation. They can be found in social situations where communication is restricted or through anonymous online interactions.

Fake people find satisfaction in causing emotional and psychological harm to others and often manipulate your words and use the information you've shared against you. Recognizing fake people early on is vital to avoid potential emotional damage. However, identifying these phony people can be challenging, especially if you interact with them occasionally or online. Seeking an outside perspective from a trusted family member or friend can help identify fake people and develop strategies to protect yourself from their damaging behaviors.

Fake people can be charming and use manipulation tactics such as guilt, flattery, and compliments to gain your approval and trust. Have a healthy skepticism when interacting with others, and don't let stereotypical gender roles influence your perception. Fake people will do whatever it takes to make you feel however they want, including exaggerating your flaws and weaknesses to make you feel inadequate and weak.

They may also treat you disrespectfully while portraying themselves as superior or ideal. Protecting your mental health and well-being is crucial by not allowing fake people to mistreat you or believe their negative opinions. Struggling teenagers can develop healthy socializing habits to avoid exposure to these phonies.

Alternative impression fake people may initially appear authentic and supportive, but their true intentions or behaviors emerge over time. They may exhibit inconsistent or unpredictable behaviors, switch between supportive and dismissive attitudes, or use manipulative tactics. These individuals can create confusion and emotional turmoil, making it challenging for teens or adults to discern their true intentions and establish stable and healthy relationships.

Over time, they'll start to shut down and distance themselves from your social group to maintain power and control over you. They may insist on controlling every aspect of your life without giving you any say. They may take control of your social life, almost acting like a boss.

For example, someone who seems nice may ask you how you're feeling in an interested manner, but be utterly calm about your well-being and not ask any follow-up questions. They may also offer you unsolicited advice and make negative judgments about you that are not based on your behavior. These individuals are very good at manipulating people, primarily when motivated by their needs and wants.

This type of person will seek to push their agenda onto others rather than genuinely care for them. They may appear to help you, but in reality, they're just trying to get someone to do their bidding. Whether or not an alternative impression fake person is completely genuine or just bluffs for the sake of power. Their inauthentic nature causes significant problems for teens struggling with depression. Initially, they may appear to be a strong supporter, but their behavior will eventually come to light. Develop strategies and habits for recognizing and avoiding these people who focus on preying on someone exhibiting a weak spirit.

It's not uncommon for people to be willing to do things for others, whether offering a helping hand or going out of their way to assist someone in need. At times, individuals may inadvertently become pawns in someone else's game, doing things for them without realizing they are being exploited. This can happen when someone is overly eager to please or has difficulty saying no. They may feel they need to do everything they can to keep others happy or avoid conflict, even if it means sacrificing their needs and desires. Unfortunately, this can create an opportunity for others to take advantage of and use them for their own benefit.

It's essential to be aware of these situations and recognize when someone is trying to use you. This can be challenging, as manipulators may be skilled at disguising their true intentions and making you feel like you're doing something of your own free will. Being aware of certain signs can help you identify if someone is using you. For instance, if you feel like you're constantly doing things for someone without receiving anything in return or sense that your boundaries are being violated, it's crucial to speak up and set limits.

Communicate your discomfort with the situation and let them know that you won't continue to do things for them if it's not mutually beneficial. Remember that it's okay to say no and prioritize your own needs, even if it means potentially upsetting someone else. By recognizing the signs of someone using you and being proactive about setting boundaries, you can protect yourself and maintain healthy relationships with others. Your kindness and willingness to help should never be taken advantage of.

Building a support system of real people who offer genuine support, understanding, and encouragement can positively impact one's mental health journey. To achieve this, be aware of the characteristics and behaviors associated with fake people. By doing so, they can avoid negative influences and prioritize relationships that promote their well-being. Teens should trust their instincts and seek authentic connections based on mutual respect, understanding, and empathy.

Engaging in activities aligning with their interests and joining support-ive communities when needed can also help teens build a network of genuine relationships that contribute positively to their mental health and recovery from depression. Overall, teenagers must prioritize their mental health and well-being by surrounding themselves with real people who offer authentic support and care. By avoiding negative influences and building healthy relationships, teens can create a robust support system that contributes positively to their mental health journey.

Maintaining Genuine Connections

Teens may struggle with connecting genuinely with others, especially if they have experienced prolonged exposure to fake people. In addition to potentially having trust issues, teens may feel uncomfortable and awkward around others due to low self-esteem and social anxiety.

You should take a particular focus on the relationship's quality rather than the quantity. Investing in meaningful relationships with individuals who share similar interests, values, experiences, and beliefs can contribute positively to their recovery from depression. This type of relationship leads to greater trust and support, which can help teens feel a sense of belonging and improve their mental health.

One way to build connections is through what each person shares. For example, teens may find a shared interest in sports, music, or art helpful for building genuine relationships. Sharing interests with others often helps build trust and allows people to relate on a more personal level. It connects two people by allowing them to feel closer together even when they don't see each other daily.

Having a genuine connection with someone who truly cares and under-stands can significantly impact recovery. It can help reduce mental health risks related to anxiety, stress, and depression. Building relationships that foster trust, giving others the benefit of the doubt, and asking for what you want without being overly demanding are all crucial skills to learn when building genuine connections. Focusing on genuinely healthy relationships makes connections beyond simple interactions based on superficial traits or interests.

Chapter Eighteen

Maintain Your Faith, Let God Hear You

Maintaining one's faith can provide a much-needed source of strength, solace, and guidance. This chapter explores the role of devotion and spirituality in navigating mental health challenges, encouraging readers to embrace their spiritual journey and find comfort in their relationship with God. Whether through prayer, meditation, scripture study, or participation in a church community, faith will help individuals find resilience, hope, and a sense of purpose amid their struggles.

While faith is a profoundly personal experience, it can serve as a steadfast anchor amidst the storms of anxiety and depression. It offers a space for reflection, introspection, and connection with something greater than oneself. Faith holds a profound power that can uplift and sustain individuals, especially during difficult times such as:

Finding Meaning and Purpose: Faith offers a sense of meaning and purpose in life, providing a broader perspective that extends beyond individual struggles. It helps individuals connect with a greater purpose, feel a sense of belonging, and find solace in knowing that their experiences are part of a larger tapestry.

Source of Comfort and Support: Belief in the Almighty can provide deep comfort and support during challenging times. Knowing that God loves and cares for you unconditionally can bring solace and a sense of being held amid emotional turmoil. The rituals, prayers, and traditions within one's faith can offer a safe space for seeking reassurance and finding strength.

Resilience and Hope: You can cultivate resilience and foster hope, even in the face of adversity. The teachings and stories within the Bible highlight stories of perseverance, strength, and overcoming hardships, serving as a source of inspiration. Instilling a belief that suffering has a purpose and that brighter days lie ahead.

Community and Connection: Engaging with a church congregation will provide a supportive network of individuals who share similar beliefs and values. This community can offer emotional support, guidance, and a sense of belonging, reducing feelings of isolation and providing a space for shared traditions, prayers, and healing practices.

Inner Peace and Spiritual Well-being: Faith nurtures inner peace and spiritual well-being by encouraging individuals to cultivate a relationship with Jesus, who paid the ultimate price for you. Individuals can find peace and connection through prayer, meditation, or other daily practices. Life is full of distractions, redirecting your focus and allowing yourself to become your best.

Understanding the power of faith allows individuals to tap into its potential benefits in supporting their mental health. By embracing the Holy Spirit as a source of strength, comfort, and resilience, individuals can navigate any challenges of anxiety and depression with a renewed sense of purpose and hope. We will explore practical strategies for nurturing and deepening one's faith and discuss ways to integrate faith with mental health support to enhance everything you are.

Nurturing Your Faith

To nurture faith, you must first obtain trust in Jesus that He was who he said He was. God's only Son, born among humanity, shared many messages with all who listened and developed a relationship with everyone throughout the years. His greatest commandment was, "You shall love the Lord your God with all your heart, and with all your soul, and with all your mind." Jesus told everyone to love one another, love your neighbor as yourself.

It's essential to actively nurture and deepen the spiritual connection. Individuals can employ His messages to promote a flourishing faith, allowing a guiding force to navigate life's challenges. By using prayer, scripture study, and reflection on what you've learned, you can acquire a more profound spiritual comfort in your faith. Here are practical strategies that can be employed to encourage and strengthen faith:

Prayer: Prayer is a direct communication to God. It can take various forms, such as formal prayers, spontaneous conversations, or silent contemplation. Regular prayer allows individuals to express their concerns, seek guidance, and find comfort in knowing they are heard and understood. Ask the Holy Spirit to guide you if you don't know what to pray or how to pray.

Meditation: Meditation offers a means of quieting the mind, finding inner peace, and deepening spiritual awareness. Through mindfulness practices, individuals can focus their attention, cultivate a sense of presence, and open themselves to spiritual insights and inspiration.

Scripture Study: Engaging with sacred texts and scriptures provides a source of guidance, wisdom, and spiritual nourishment. Reading and studying scriptures, whether independently or in a group setting, allows individuals to explore the teachings of their faith, gain insights, and apply these teachings to their daily lives. Jesus is called the "Alpha and Omega," which means the beginning and the end. This title emphasizes that Jesus is the eternal God who existed before the world's creation and will continue to exist long after the end of time. The Book of Revelation in the Bible refers to Jesus as the Alpha and Omega, highlighting His role as the one who holds all power and authority and is the ultimate source of salvation and redemption for all humanity. Essentially, this title signifies that Jesus is the origin and the ultimate goal of all things, and everything exists for his glory and purpose.

Reflection and Journaling: Taking time with a Christian daily devotion book can be valuable for recording thoughts, prayers, and wisdom, enabling a personal connection.

Engaging with a Faith Community: Actively participating in a community of believers provides worship and fellowship opportunities. Attending services, joining study groups or prayer circles, and engaging in community service activities are the best worship experiences.

Seeking Guidance from Religious Leaders: Religious leaders, such as pastors, priests, or spiritual mentors, can offer guidance, support, and insights into navigating the challenges of faith and mental health. Seeking their counsel and participating in spiritual counseling sessions can provide valuable lessons and reassurance. With today's technology, you can view nearly any church service you want from the internet or many television stations. By employing these practical strategies, individuals can nurture their faith. We will address the potential challenges that may arise in maintaining confidence during periods of anxiety or depression and offer suggestions for overcoming them.

Letting God Hear You

Prayer is the most powerful tool; by understanding how to let God hear your prayers, individuals can develop a closer relationship and find comfort in knowing they are not alone in their struggles.

The Essence of Prayer: A prayer is a sacred act of communication, whether it's through spoken words, silent contemplation, or written expressions. It provides a means of expressing one's deepest thoughts, fears, hopes, and desires. Through prayer, individuals can seek guidance, find comfort, and cultivate a sense of connection with something greater than themselves.

Different Forms of Prayer: Prayer can take various forms, allowing individuals to find any way they choose to speak with God.

Spontaneous prayers allow individuals to express their initial thoughts and emotions in their own words, providing a more personal and intimate connection with the Lord Almighty. Silent prayer or contemplation enables individuals to cultivate stillness and listen to the whispers of the divine within their hearts. Many people find comfort and strength in praying throughout the day. Whether a quick prayer of gratitude or a more extended prayer asking for guidance and support, connecting with God helps individuals feel grounded and centered. Prayer can serve as a reminder of one's faith and the presence of a higher power, providing a feeling of reassurance and yearning during great moments and hardships.

Honesty and Vulnerability in Prayer: Authenticity and vulnerability are essential in prayer. It's important to approach prayer with a genuine and open heart, expressing one's true thoughts and emotions without judgment or pretense. Letting go of any fears of being judged and trusting in His unconditional love and understanding allows individuals to fully express themselves and find relief in the presence of divine reality.

Listening and Finding Guidance: Prayer is not just about speaking but also about listening. It creates space for silence to become receptive, allowing individuals to feel divine guidance as they read God's inspired words throughout the Bible. Paying attention to one's intuition, insights, and signs from one's experience can provide a sense of guidance and direction during times of anxiety and depression. Especially when things don't go as planned, life's struggles and failures allow you to improve every moment in your future.

Prayer in Community: While personal prayer is essential, community worship offers collective strength and support. Participating in group prayers, prayer circles, or spiritual services fosters a sense of unity, strengthens holy reinforcement, and provides a shared spiritual experience. Harmony of the mind will help you reach your goals because you'll desire to be a better person. Strengthen your faith and find comfort, stability, and direction by allowing God to hear you through prayer.

Integrating Faith and Mental Health

By developing a personal prayer practice cultivating authenticity and vulnerability, individuals can experience transformative energy.

Recognizing the Complementary Roles: Faith and mental health can work synergistically by providing spiritual guidance, a sense of purpose, and comfort in times of distress. Integrating faith becomes amazing when ingrained in everything you do.

At the same time, being part of a church community can offer valuable support, including interventions, counseling, and redirection when necessary. By acknowledging and appreciating the overall support that is available, individuals can access the holistic care that they need. It's essential to engage in conversations about maintaining solid viewpoints and the role they play in personal healing. Sharing personal experiences, concerns, and opinions can help create a collaborative approach that incorporates one's own confidence and the support of the church community.

Addressing Spiritual Concerns: Individuals may have spiritual concerns, such as questioning their faith, feeling distant from God, or struggling with spiritual practices. Seek guidance from church leadership who can provide spiritual counsel, address spiritual questions, and offer perspectives that align with one's faith. Mental health professionals can also support individuals in exploring and reconciling their spiritual beliefs within the context of their mental health journey.

Holistic Well-Being: Embracing is recognizing that life's mental, emotional, and spiritual aspects are interconnected. Engage in self-care practices that nurture mental health and faith, such as maintaining a healthy lifestyle, engaging in spiritual practices, seeking support from faith communities, and cultivating meaningful relationships. People are commonly dissatisfied with specific areas of life, especially compared to others. Take time to appreciate the moments, be thankful for what you have, and honestly, be grateful for what you don't have. Understand some things can be scary and different. Even if you fail, it's how you get yourself back up and improve your surroundings.

Supportive Faith Communities: Seek out ministries and support groups, as you will find compassionate and empathetic individuals wherever God has left His mark. Hundreds of people around you may be going through something similar to your struggles, and you are never alone in your journey. Remember that God is greater than anything you might face, and you're not alone in your experiences. Life is not always easy, and there may be bumps along the way. However, realize that everything is temporary, and as a believer in the Almighty, you can find ways to praise and give thanks during moments of joy and during challenging times.

Holding onto Hope

In the face of depression, holding hope becomes essential for resilience and healing. Faith-based practices offer powerful tools to cultivate hope and renew strength during challenging times. This section will explore the significance of holding onto hope and provide practical strategies to nurture hope through faith.

The Power of Hope: Hope is a beacon of light that illuminates the path through dark times. It instills optimism, fuels motivation, and allows individuals to envision a brighter future. Holding onto hope provides a sense of purpose, reminding individuals that their current struggles are not permanent and that healing and transformation are possible. By maintaining a positive focus, you can pull yourself out of anything.

Finding Comfort in Spiritual Teachings: Biblical stories always contain teachings and accounts that inspire hope. Exploring and meditating on Jesus' instructions can provide relief and reinforce His compassion. Reflect on stability, miracles, and stories for strength and encouragement. It's very comforting knowing Jesus conquered the world and promised to make a place for each one who accepts Him as Savior.

Practicing Gratitude: Fostering hope can be achieved by cultivating a positive attitude of gratitude. Engage in regular gratitude practices, such as keeping a gratitude journal or offering prayers of appreciation, to recognize and appreciate life's small or significant blessings. Gratitude helps shift the focus from challenges to the positive aspects, nurturing hope and fostering a sense of abundance. Remember, as you grow older, God can give and take away. Believing in God's power can help you overcome obstacles of any size. No matter how big or small your problems seem, you can always count on God to listen and provide assistance.

Connecting with Supportive Faith Community: Surrounding oneself with a supportive faith community is vital for cultivating hope. Engage in meaningful connections with individuals who uplift, encourage, and share a similar faith perspective. Participate in group activities, attend religious services, and join support groups that provide an environment of empathy, understanding, and shared hope.

Drawing Strength from Spiritual Practices: Spiritual practices can provide hope and renewal. Prayer, meditation, scripture study, and reflection offer moments of connection with a higher power and allow for deep introspection. These practices provide opportunities to release burdens, gain clarity, and find solace in the presence of a divine presence.

The Bible, assembled and maintained over the years, is an excellent source of guidance for Christians. It contains accounts of how God created and led His people throughout history. By studying the Bible and reflecting on its historical credibility, individuals can gain a deeper understanding of God's plan and how it can be applied to their own lives. Connect with God and reflect on His strength.

By focusing on God's power and asking for His help and guidance, individuals can find strength and inspiration to face the challenges of life. Talk with people who have overcome significant adversity through their faith or observing the beauty and wonder of the natural world. By sharing experiences and insights with others, individuals can gain new perspectives on God's strength and find inspiration to deepen their faith.

Seeking Divine Guidance: Surrendering worries and anxieties to a higher power through prayer can bring relief and hope. Trust that a compassionate higher power is listening and guiding the way. Seek guidance, wisdom, and clarity through prayer and trust in the answers that come, even if they may not align with immediate expectations. Waiting for prayers to be answered can be a challenging experience for many people. Maintaining faith and hope during waiting periods can be difficult, especially if the outcome is uncertain.

However, there are several ways that people can cope with waiting for prayers to be answered. Patience is a fundamental virtue when waiting for prayers to be answered. Trusting that God has a plan for our lives and will answer our prayers in His time and in His way is essential. Practicing patience can help us maintain faith and hope, even in the face of uncertainty. Continuing to pray, even when waiting for answers, it'll help us find comfort and strength in His presence. Praying can also help us clarify our thoughts and feelings and identify what we truly want and need.

One inspiring Bible story that illustrates the importance of patience and waiting for prayers to be answered is in the Old Testament. In Daniel chapter 10, we read about Daniel, who prayed and fasting for three weeks, seeking guidance and understanding from God. Daniel had been mourning and abstaining from delicacies, wine, and meat during this time. He was deeply troubled by a vision he had received and sought God's help in understanding its meaning. Finally, after three weeks of persistent prayer, an angel appeared to Daniel, explaining the importance of his vision and revealing God's plan for the future. The angel told Daniel that he had been sent in response to his prayers but had been delayed by a spiritual battle with the prince of Persia.

This illustrates the importance of patience in waiting for prayers to be answered. Although Daniel had to wait for three weeks to receive an answer from God, he maintained his faith and trust in God throughout this time. He continued to pray and seek God's guidance, even when he did not receive an immediate answer. Daniel's patience and perseverance were rewarded, and he received a powerful message. We must wait patiently for God's answers to our prayers and trust in His plan, even when we do not understand the reasons for the delay.

By holding onto hope and integrating faith-based practices into daily life, individuals can find strength, resilience, and a renewed sense of purpose. Through gratitude, affirmations, connecting with a supportive faith community, and drawing power from spiritual practices, individuals can foster hope even during anxiety and depression. Remember, your faith is a steadfast companion on this journey, offering support, inspiration, and a sense of purpose. You need to grow as a person by avoiding procrastination, believing in yourself and desire something better. As you move forward, may your faith continue to guide you, empower you, and bring you closer to a place of peace and healing.

Chapter Nineteen

Building a Positive Future

A dolescents often experience pressure from schoolwork and various obligations. One way to combat the effects of anxiety and depression in teenagers is by cultivating a positive lifestyle. A single moment can profoundly impact your life, whether it's a small act of kindness or a life decision. While positive moments can help shape your thoughts and habits, fueling positive energy often requires hard work and making choices that align with your goals.

This process can range from striving for personal growth to making decisions that positively impact those around you. Building a positive life isn't limited to teenagers; anyone can achieve a brighter future with dedication and perseverance. Amidst the mounting pressure of daily life, God has a greater purpose for your life. This purpose is rooted not only in your personal achievements but in the love and support you offer to others. God's plan for you extends beyond the challenges of anxiety, depression, and stress and encompasses a life filled with hope and meaning.

It's not uncommon to face challenging times that appear to be never-ending. These are the moments when God works to strengthen our character. In moments of hopelessness, remember that God has a plan for us and a reason for placing us on this earth, even during difficult times. By understanding that our lives have purpose and meaning, we can overcome adversity and learn to live in the present moment.

Life's challenging moments are opportunities for personal growth and development, shaping us into the person God intends us to be. Rather than being overwhelmed by anxiety, focus on the happiness that God brings to your life daily. In First Corinthians 10:13, "No temptation has overtaken you that is not common to man. God is faithful, and He will not let you be tempted beyond your ability, but with the temptation, He will also provide the way of escape, that you may be able to endure it." (ESV)

Temptations are often associated with external influences that compel us to do something destructive. These challenges are usually more complex and can arise within ourselves. We must prioritize our desire for God over our personal detrimental actions to overcome these temptations. We can choose to follow Christ and his teachings or continue down a path of self-destruction. Rather than succumbing to life's pressures, we can seek guidance from God to navigate complex decisions and challenges.

Diamonds are formed under immense pressure; similarly, moments of hardship can be powerful opportunities for transformation. It's not about what one possesses but rather how one utilizes their knowledge to overcome obstacles and cultivate positivity. How one responds to adversity accurately benchmarks character and maturity potential. Situations don't define an individual but provide another opportunity to overcome the barriers and become stronger. Everyone experiences difficulties and dark moments in life, but by facing challenges with courage and determination, you can emerge as a new creation and the best version of yourself.

Taking responsibility for yourself is a crucial step towards achieving a positive life. Instead of focusing on complaints or worries, focus on taking action to improve your situation. It's all too easy to blame external factors or other people for our problems, but this only perpetuates a cycle of negativity and powerlessness. When we take ownership of our lives, we empower ourselves to make meaningful changes and create a better future. This means acknowledging that we have agency and control over our thoughts, actions, and decisions. We can't control everything that happens to us, but we can control how we respond to our scenarios.

Feeling overwhelmed or discouraged is natural, but it's important not to give up or expect things to fix themselves. Instead, approach challenges with a proactive and solutions-oriented mindset. Identifying the problem, brainstorming potential solutions, and taking action to implement the changes will lead to victory. While it can be tempting to play the blame game, this ultimately does more harm than good. Blaming others or external factors for our problems only absolves us of responsibility and perpetuates a victim mentality. By owning our lives and taking responsibility for our actions, we become more resilient, self-sufficient, and empowered.

God desires our lives to be filled with happiness and meaning, providing us the opportunity to create a positive future. Remain strong to overcome any obstacles that threaten to take away your joy. When considering the future, it's easy to believe that life will improve once you enter college or secure a job. The good news is that change is possible but requires steps to make it happen.

One way to build a positive future is by planning for what you want. It doesn't have to be perfectly written; outline your desires and list what needs to play out for your plan to succeed. By knowing what you want and how to get there, you can build a better tomorrow and overcome everything in your way. Think about your life now and how you would like it to be in the future. Where do you see yourself in 5 years? Ten years? What makes that period so different from now, and how can you make it happen? This is a great way to develop goals for your future because it provides a transparent vision of where your life should be headed. To have a positive future, have a game plan to take you there because seeing is believing.

Building goals allows you to form a path toward hope and inspiration. Declaring your intention and making it known is a way to ensure you will maintain motivation. You can express your choices to friends and family, but once you do, remember all those around you will watch your ambitions come to life. When your goals are laid out, it'll give you the strength and willpower to build on them every day of your life. It's truly remarkable when, deep down, you establish a mission statement, you have a heading and a map, and you slowly set your course while seeking your destination. The secret to life's success is selling yourself on your idea; anything can happen whenever you believe in yourself.

Going through this process of imagination and declaration of intentions, your path toward a positive future is more certain than ever. You can ensure your success and happiness by implementing these steps. So, what is it that you want? Once you figure it out, you can start working to make it happen. As a teen, you have many choices in life. You have more options now than the youth did 20 years ago. You may not be able to handle some decisions quite yet, and it could fuel anxiety. When we see different paths in front of us and don't know which one to take, imagining the consequences in either direction can be scary.

When you're humble and feel your place in life, you can take a calm approach and avoid being stressed out. It's not about being weak or being a pushover; it's about making positive choices in life, choices that move you toward your goals and give you a better life for your future. When you are selfless and think about others on your way, it'll help you find success in everything you do. You can build an optimistic destiny by showing love and compassion for others around you. Not only will they appreciate your kindness, but this habit can help you develop self-confidence and pride in yourself.

When you're confident and secure in who you are, it's easier to make the right choices. You'll be strong enough to stand up for yourself and those around you, even if that means facing tough challenges or overcoming impossible hurdles. When people see your positivity and love, they will be inspired to do the same thing. A cycle of positivity starts when one person takes a step forward. If you can do this for yourself, it will inspire others to do the same thing for their lives.

During problematic times, it's easy to feel overwhelmed and alone. You may find yourself struggling with negative thoughts and emotions, which can be highly stressful. Remember that you're not alone. Look around and identify the people in your life who matter most. These individuals can give you the support and encouragement needed to overcome challenges and cultivate a positive future. Remember, when we help one another, everyone benefits.

By improving our lives through positivity and love, we can inspire others to do the same. The support we receive from others cannot be measured by material possessions; it's priceless. It can make all the difference in the world. We can find ourselves in a much better place with the proper support. Even small acts of kindness can have a snowball effect, leading to more positivity in our lives. So, allow positivity to enter your life and keep rolling it forward.

For example, gaining wisdom and knowledge from all those around you can significantly impact your confidence when facing life's challenges. It can also alter your perspective towards situations, leading to a more positive outlook and life-changing results. It's the small things that make a big difference. When someone supports you, it's truly appreciated, and you realize how much they mean to you. Wise influences show us how to navigate tricky situations without anxiety or fear. Having someone to talk to and rely on makes it easier to overcome any obstacle that life throws our way. We can avoid being dragged down by the negativity of the world and instead rely on the kindness of others.

Although some people may want to hurt others, recognize them for who they are and not let their negativity affect us. To truly understand the people in our lives, we must look beyond their words and actions and seek the truth. The truth is always out there, and how we choose to react to each obstacle is entirely up to us. Negative characteristics can make it difficult for others to believe in us, especially if they don't give us the benefit of the doubt. However, when others know about our positive qualities and the changes we've made, they will desire to be closer to you, as everyone wants positivity.

God can form and mold you like clay or chisel you into perfection by guiding you through life's challenges and obstacles. Just like a potter molds and shapes clay into a beautiful vessel, God can shape and transform you into the person He desires you to be. Similarly, as a sculptor chisels away at a block of marble to create a masterpiece, God can chisel away at the parts of your life that need refining, molding you into a better version of yourself. God can use your trials and hardships to strengthen your character and build your faith, ultimately transforming you into who He created you to be. Trust in God's plan for your life and allow Him to shape you, just like the potter with clay or a sculptor with marble example.

Chapter Twenty

The Power of Positive Affirmations

L et's face it, everyone has bad days. As a teenager, you might have more than your fair share, as your life seems to be a whirlwind of emotional, physical, and social changes. The world appears vast and overwhelming, and you might sometimes feel like you're battling the unknowns. But here's the big secret: you possess a superpower that can help you navigate these choppy waters. This superpower is your mind, precisely the words and phrases I'm about to tell you. These are known as affirmations, and they can change your world.

Affirmations are like software programs for the mind, continually running in the background, shaping our feelings, actions, and, ultimately, our reality. Think of your mind as a garden. The thoughts you think are the seeds you plant, and the affirmations are the watering and nourishment that allows those seeds to grow. If you tend to your garden with care and positivity, the flowers bloom beautifully, but if you let weeds of negative thoughts overtake you, the garden's beauty diminishes. Our grandparents and great-grandparents understood all about weeds and the importance of removing them whenever possible.

You don't forfeit your garden to weeds! Whenever you want to become strong and powerful, go outside, find the weeds, and start pulling them. Getting your hands dirty and working hard in all you do it'll give you a sense of pride. Knowing you won't allow nonsense and you're willing to cultivate your life.

Neuroscientists have discovered a feature of the brain called neuroplasticity, which is the ability of the brain to alter its fundamental structure and functions in response to experiences. This means that the more you repeat a particular thought or behavior, the stronger the neural pathways for that thought or behavior become.

Think of it like a trail in the woods. The more you walk down a particular path, the clearer and more defined it becomes. The same goes for your brain. Repeating positive affirmations makes those positive thought pathways more precise and defined, making it easier for your brain to access and use them. This can help you counter the negative thought patterns often associated with anxiety and depression.

Creating affirmations is a personal and creative process. The most effective declarations resonate with you and reflect the change you want to see in yourself and your life. Here are some tips to help you craft your affirmations:

Make it Personal: Your affirmation should be about you and no one else. Make it personal and intimate. Instead of saying, "People are kind to me," say, "I deserve kindness and receive it from others."

Use Present Tense: Phrase your affirmation as though it has already happened. This helps your brain to act as if the desired change has already occurred, motivating you to make that change happen. Instead of saying, "I will be confident," say, "I am confident."

Stay Positive: This one might seem obvious, but it's essential. Affirmations should focus on what you want rather than what you don't want. Rather than saying, "I'm not anxious," say, "I am calm and in control."

Keep it Simple and Clear: Your affirmations should be easy to remember and repeat. Keep the language straightforward and the message clear.

Consistency is Key: Make a routine of repeating your affirmations. You could do this when you wake up before bed or at any other time during the day when you can spare a few quiet moments.

Believe in Them: The words will only make a difference if you feel the emotion behind them. They will only be effective if you believe in your commitments.

Visualize It: When repeating your affirmations, visualize what the statement means. For example, if your assertion is "I am confident," imagine yourself standing tall and proud, speaking confidently, and feeling secure in who you are.

Write Them Down: Keep a journal of your affirmations. Writing them down can make them feel more natural, and you can also track how your feelings and beliefs change over time.

Be Patient: Changes won't happen overnight. Remember, you're trying to overwrite long-standing thought patterns. This takes time, so be patient with yourself.

If you're having trouble coming up with affirmations, here are a few to get you started:

"I am enough; nobody is going to hold me back."

"Every day, I am becoming stronger and more resilient."

"I am in control of my emotions; they do not control me."

"I choose peace and positivity over anxiety and fear."

"I am worthy of love, happiness, and success."

"I embrace my journey and will celebrate my progress."

"I am not my mistakes; I'll learn and grow from them."

"I trust in my ability to face challenges and overcome them."

"I am filled with gratitude for the good in my life."

"I love and accept myself unconditionally."

These affirmations begin a mental shift as a stepping stone toward a more positive mindset. They can act as a powerful antidote against negative thoughts and self-doubt. Not every affirmation will resonate with you, and that's okay. The power of a commitment comes from its relevance. Choose words and phrases that ring true to you and make you feel uplifted, empowered, and at peace.

Customizing your affirmations to fit your unique personality and situation can make them even more powerful. For instance, if you're dealing with social anxiety, an affirmation like, "I am comfortable and confident in social situations," can be helpful. If you're struggling with self-esteem, a statement such as, "I'm valuable, and my thoughts and feelings matter," can help bolster your self-worth. As your needs and circumstances change, your affirmations can evolve with you. Remember, nothing is set in stone. They're flexible, dynamic tools that can adapt to your growth and transformation.

Making affirmations part of your daily routine is the most effective way to reap their benefits. Here are some ways you can incorporate them into your life:

Affirmation Journals: Writing affirmations in a dedicated journal reinforces them and allows you to reflect on your progress over time. As you review your entries, you'll see your growth and how your thoughts have evolved, which can be very empowering.

Affirmation Art: If you enjoy being creative, turning your affirmations into art can be a fun and effective practice. This could be anything from painting them on a canvas, writing them in beautiful calligraphy, or even creating a digital design. For years, people never knew what they were doing. They doodled, drew something, and painted; in reality, everything was an outward expression of an inward feeling.

Meditation and Affirmation: Combining your affirmations with regular meditation can benefit you. During meditation, your mind is open and receptive, making it an ideal time to introduce positive affirmations.

Affirmation Reminders: This is the most popular choice. Place sticky notes with affirmations on your mirror, laptop, or any place you regularly see them. These can serve as little reminders to maintain a positive mindset throughout the day.

Remember, the main aim of positive affirmations is to empower you. It's about reprogramming your brain to foster self-love, courage, and resilience. It's a pathway to seeing yourself in a new, brighter light and embracing the undeniable fact that you are capable, worthy, and enough.

Positive Affirmations: These positive statements reinforce hopeful beliefs and encourage a positive mindset. Create personal affirmations that align with Godly values and use them as daily reminders of hope and resilience. Repeat them regularly, internalize their meaning, and allow them to shape thoughts and actions.

1. "I am fearfully and wonderfully made by God."

2. "I trust in God's plan for my life, and I know that everything will work out for my good."

3. "I am capable of achieving great things through God's strength."

4. "I am loved unconditionally by God, and nothing can ever change that."

5. "I have the love of Christ and can love others according to His will."

6. "I am blessed with the peace that surpasses all understanding through my faith in God."

7. "I am forgiven by God for my mistakes and shortcomings, and I am free to move forward in His grace."

8. "I am surrounded by God's love, protection, and guidance every moment of every day."

9. "I am grateful for the blessings that God has given me, and I will use them for His glory."

10. "I am a child of God, and He has a unique purpose and calling for my life."

Chapter Twenty–One

Rewiring Your Thoughts

Teenagers are often seen as entitled, thinking that they deserve everything without putting in the effort. This behavior can lead to problems in both their personal and professional lives. The root of entitlement in teenagers is often linked to their upbringing, as they may have been raised with overindulgence and low expectations. One of the main issues with entitled teenagers is that they tend to lack empathy for others. They may not be aware of their behavior's impact on those around them and may not care about others' feelings. This can lead to them being selfish and self-centered.

Another issue with entitled teenagers is that they may not take responsibility for their actions. They may blame others for their mistakes rather than admit fault and learn from their experiences. This leads to a need for more personal growth and development. Entitled teenagers may also struggle with setting and achieving goals. They may feel a lack of motivation and direction in life. In addition, entitled teenagers may struggle with relationships. They may have difficulty maintaining friendships and romantic relationships because they may not be willing to compromise or put in the effort required for a healthy relationship.

It takes time to accomplish everything; life isn't about snapping your fingers and expecting everything to go as planned. Teens struggle in the workplace; they have unrealistic expectations about their job responsibilities, pay, and advancement opportunities. They may also need help taking constructive criticism and may not be willing to work hard to succeed in their careers. So, why do teenagers feel entitled?

There are many possible reasons, including overindulgence by parents, unrealistic societal expectations, and a lack of consequences for bad behavior. In some cases, entitled behavior may also result from mental health issues derived from anxiety or depression. Parents and educators must set clear expectations and boundaries to combat entitlement in teenagers. Teenagers must understand that they are not entitled to everything and must work hard to achieve their passions.

Parents should also avoid overindulging their children and teach them the value of hard work and responsibility. Teenagers need to develop empathy and communication skills. They need to be aware of how their behavior impacts others and should be willing to listen and compromise in relationships. Developing these skills can help teenagers succeed in their personal and professional lives. They should be encouraged to learn from their mistakes and to work hard to improve themselves.

Develop a positive mindset and become more resilient in facing challenges. A new generation is on its way; mental strength, wisdom, and learning from history are necessary for the future to be bright. However, by setting clear expectations, developing empathy and communication skills, and teaching the importance of responsibility, parents and educators can help teenagers overcome this behavior and become successful adults. It'll be a sad day as each teen thinks it's everyone else's job to walk side by side in all the adventures.

Handling Conflicts of Mind

Handling conflicts of the mind can be a challenging issue. Adolescence is a time of significant physical and mental change, which can lead to confusion and conflicting emotions. Teenagers must learn how to manage these conflicts effectively to avoid negative consequences. One of the most common conflicts of the mind teenagers face is the struggle between fitting in and being true to themselves. Teenagers often feel pressure to conform to societal norms and expectations, which can lead to them suppressing their true feelings and desires. This can result in feelings of unhappiness, anxiety, and even depression. It's crucial for teenagers to learn how to balance fitting in with being true to themselves and to understand that it's okay to be different.

Another common conflict of the mind is the struggle between instant gratification and long-term goals. Teens often prioritize short-term plea-sure over long-term success, leading to poor decision-making and regret. Teenagers must learn to delay gratification and focus on long-term goals, even when life is challenging. Teenagers may also experience conflicts of the mind when it comes to relationships. They may struggle with balancing their needs and desires with their partner or friends, leading to misunder-standings and someone getting their feelings hurt.

It's essential for teenagers to learn how to communicate effectively and to compromise when necessary to maintain healthy relationships. Another conflict of the mind that will always be faced is the struggle between following their passions and meeting the expectations of others. Parents or teachers may pressure teenagers to pursue a specific career or academic path, even if it doesn't align with their interests or passions. It is vital for teenagers to learn how to advocate for themselves and to pursue their passions, even if it goes against the expectations of others.

Finally, teenagers may experience mind conflicts regarding their self-image and self-esteem. They may struggle with negative self-talk and feelings of inadequacy. Learn how to practice self-compassion and focus on strengths and abilities. Teenagers should develop healthy coping mechanisms to handle conflicts of the mind effectively. This may include practicing mindfulness, self-reflection, and seeking support from trusted adults or mental health professionals.

It's also vital for parents and educators to create a supportive and non-judgmental environment where teenagers feel comfortable discussing their thoughts and feelings. Conflicts of the mind can be a challenging issue for teenagers to handle. By learning how to balance fitting in with being true to themselves, delaying gratification, communicating effectively, advocating for themselves, and practicing self-compassion, teenagers can develop the skills to manage these conflicts and become resilient adults.

The Brain is a Sponge

As teenagers navigate through the tumultuous waters of adolescence, they are exposed to a vast array of experiences and stimuli that can profoundly impact their developing brains. From social media and pop culture to news and current events, the teenage brain is constantly bombarded with positive and negative information. While some of this information can be beneficial, helping teenagers to learn and grow, many potential pitfalls are associated with how teenagers see things.

One of the most significant issues with teenagers visualizing everything is that their brains are still developing and maturing during adolescence, making it difficult for teenagers to make the best choices. This can be particularly problematic regarding sinful social media experiences, where teenagers may be exposed to constant negative messages and images that can influence their self-esteem and self-image. Another issue with teenagers witnessing crowds is that they are often more susceptible to peer pressure than adults. Teens might engage in certain destructive behaviors to fit in with peers, such as drug and alcohol use, which can have serious consequences.

This is compounded by the fact that teenagers are often limited to accurately assessing risk, meaning they may need to fully understand the dangers associated with certain behaviors. You can guarantee everybody is exposed to conflicting messages. For example, while parents and teachers may encourage teenagers to make good choices and prioritize their education, popular culture may convey that it's more important to be popular and well-liked. This can lead to confusion and conflicting emotions, making it difficult for teenagers to know precisely what to focus on. In addition to these issues, many other potential concerns are associated with how teenagers see things.

Depression due to social media can be particularly damaging, given the sensitive nature of the teenage brain. So, what can be done to address these issues and help teenagers navigate through the challenges of adolescence? One possible solution is to focus on education and awareness by teaching teenagers about the dangers associated with things like scams, artificial relationships, and being used. We can help them make better choices and develop healthier habits.

Additionally, by encouraging teenagers to seek support from trusted adults, we can help them build a strong support network that can help them during difficult times. Another potential solution is to focus on regulation and moderation. While it may not be realistic to expect teenagers to avoid social media and other potentially problematic stimuli altogether, we can encourage them to use these things in moderation and take breaks when necessary. We can also work to regulate the content that teenagers are exposed to, ensuring they are not being bombarded with negative messages and images that could damage their mental health.

Ultimately, the key to addressing the issues with teenagers seeing things is to adopt a holistic approach that considers this population's unique needs and challenges. By recognizing the importance of education, awareness, regulation, and support, we can help teenagers navigate the challenges of adolescence and emerge as resilient, well-adjusted adults. While there will always be challenges associated with how teenagers see things, we can help them overcome these challenges and thrive by working together.

What it Means to Value Yourself

Getting caught up in the opinions and expectations of those around you can be easy. You may feel pressure to fit in, to be popular, or to excel in certain areas. However, it's essential to remember that external factors do not determine your worth. You are valuable simply because you exist, and you must value yourself and your unique qualities. One of the first steps in loving yourself is recognizing your strengths and talents. Take some time to reflect on what you are good at and what you enjoy doing. Do not focus your life around what your boyfriend or girlfriend is driving toward. Everyone has their own goals and ambitions; yours will be different than most of theirs.

These could be anything from playing an instrument to being an excellent listener to having a great sense of humor. By acknowledging and celebrating your strengths, you are affirming your worth as a person. It can be challenging to say no to others, especially when you want to please them or avoid conflict. However, prioritize your needs as an individual. Just because one day someone is planning to attend a particular college it doesn't mean you have to follow along unless this is also your ambition. This means learning to say no when necessary and communicating your boundaries clearly and assertively. When you respect your limits, you send a message that your time, energy, and feelings are valuable. Self-care is also a key component of valuing yourself. This can take many forms, such as getting enough sleep, eating nutritious food, exercising regularly, and engaging in activities that bring you joy.

Taking care of your physical self is a way of honoring and recognizing your worth. It's also important to surround yourself with people who value and support you. This includes friends, family members, mentors, and other positive influences in your life. Seek respectful, caring, and supportive relationships, and avoid toxic or harmful ones. By surrounding yourself with positive people, you are reinforcing your values and worth as a person. Remember that valuing yourself is an ongoing process. Sometimes, you doubt yourself or struggle with negative thoughts and emotions. However, prioritizing your well-being and affirming your worth can build a strong foundation. Value yourself, and others will follow suit.

You Stopped Yourself

Teens navigate the complexities of growing up; they often encounter situations that require them to set goals for themselves. Whether getting good grades in school, making a sports team, or landing a part-time job, setting goals is integral to personal growth and development. However, it's not uncommon for teenagers to talk themselves out of pursuing a dream because they don't believe they can accomplish it. This type of negative self-talk can harm one's self-esteem and overall well-being.

When teenagers talk themselves out of pursuing a goal, they give up before they even start. Over time, this negative self-talk can erode one's confidence and make it even harder to set and achieve future goals. Teenagers must recognize that they can fulfill their purposes and should not let self-doubt hold them back. By practicing positive self-talk and focusing on their strengths and abilities, teenagers can build the confidence and resilience to pursue their goals with determination and perseverance. One of the most effective ways to overcome negative self-talk is to re-frame one's mindset. Instead of focusing on what they can't do, teenagers should focus on what they can do.

For example, if a teenager wants to make the school basketball team but doesn't think they have the skills, they should focus on the steps they can take to improve their basketball skills. This might include practicing daily, working with a coach or mentor, and studying game footage to identify areas for improvement. Teenagers can build momentum and progress toward their goals by focusing on what they can do rather than what they can't do.

Another critical aspect of overcoming negative self-talk is surrounding oneself with positive influences. This might include friends, family members, teachers, coaches, or mentors who offer encouragement, support, and constructive feedback. By surrounding oneself with positive influences, teenagers can build a support network to stay motivated and focused on their goals. Learn how to take calculated risks to achieve goals; everything comes with pros and cons. Be willing to climb the ladder of life. Setting and achieving goals requires a certain level of risk-taking, as there is always the possibility of failure or rejection. However, taking calculated risks can help teenagers build confidence and resilience and develop essential life skills such as problem-solving, decision-making, and adaptability.

When taking risks, teenagers need to evaluate the potential consequences and develop a plan for managing any adverse outcomes. This might include setting realistic expectations, seeking advice and support from trusted individuals, and creating a backup plan if things don't go as planned. By taking calculated risks and learning from successes and failures, teenagers can build the skills and confidence to pursue their goals with determination and perseverance. Remembering how teens talk themselves out of a plan cannot be overstated. Don't let self-doubt hold you back from reaching your full potential.

How Many Times Do You Give Up

Persistence is a critical factor in achieving success in science and life. How often have you given up on a goal, regretting it later? Perhaps you convinced yourself that you couldn't reach it or that it was too difficult or time-consuming. Whatever the reason, it's important to remember that giving up should never be the first option. Instead, we should strive to find new approaches, seek a new angle, and learn all we can to tackle those objectives. In the world of science, persistence is significant. Researchers and scientists often spend years conducting experiments and analyzing data without guaranteeing success. However, they understand that the path to discovery is rarely straightforward. Some of the most groundbreaking findings in history have resulted from trial and error, perseverance, and a willingness to try new things.

Everything requires a willingness to keep trying despite setbacks and obstacles. In our personal lives, persistence is just as important. Whether we're working towards a professional goal, a personal passion, or a relationship, it's important to remember that success rarely comes easily. We may encounter setbacks, rejection, and disappointment, but experiences are valuable to learning new opportunities. Arm yourself with knowledge, plan to acquire skills you desire to know, and seek opportunities to gain more experience. Eventually, your persistence pays off, and you're headed in your chosen direction.

There are a few times in life when people bite more than they can chew; giving up may be the best option. For example, suppose a goal no longer aligns with your time limits and finances, causing significant stress. In that case, reevaluate that goal for another moment in time and make a different short-term choice. However, even in these situations, it's essential to approach the decision with intention and thoughtfulness rather than simply giving up out of fear or frustration.

Persistence is a critical factor in achieving success in science and life. Giving up and moving on to something else can be tempting when faced with setbacks, rejection, or difficulties. However, we can overcome obstacles and achieve our goals by embracing persistence, seeking new approaches, and learning from failure. Remember, success isn't instant, but it's always within reach for those willing to keep trying. Some ideas may require a long-term commitment; other goals might be in your window of opportunity right now.

Chapter Twenty-Two

Mentorship

In 2022, after working in the hospital setting for years, I was willing to try new things. I grew up reading books and desired to be an author one day. My children and I focused on ideas; we drafted over 24 canine characters and personalities and started making stories. In January 2023, I launched a children's book series called Poochville! Then the books Super Powers, Shoes, Tackle the Chores, Walls, Nikki Comes Home, K-9 Tournament, Rivals, and many others were hitting the market. See your goals, feel them, and watch your dreams come true!

The Coach Story

A coach had a conversation with a student struggling with motivation and commitment. After practice, the student approached the coach and asked if he could skip a few drills. He didn't want to give his all during training; he avoided challenges and responsibilities. He told the coach that he just wanted to get through the day and be done with it. The coach listened to him carefully, then replied firmly: "You will never amount to anything unless you give life your all and be dedicated to all you do." Surprised, the student looked at the coach, realizing displaying your all takes more than giving a little. Life is complex; you'll only achieve your goals if you give your all.

The coach understood what he was going through, but giving up was not the answer. He reminded the student of the importance of setting and working toward goals, even when things get complicated. Then, he explained that he was only setting himself up for failure by avoiding challenges and responsibilities. The student listened to the coach and then asked how to find the motivation to keep going. The coach replied that inspiration comes from within, and it's up to him to discover what will impact his life the most.

Some ideas were suggested about what he wants to achieve and then breaking that goal into smaller, achievable steps. The coach told him to focus on the process, not the outcome, and to celebrate the small victories along the way while reminding him of the importance of having a support system. The coach told him to surround himself with team members who believed in him and would encourage him to keep going, even when things got tough. The coach emphasized that nothing had to be done alone. Asking for help was a sign of strength, not weakness. As the conversation ended, there was a glimmer of hope in the players' eyes. He thanked the coach for taking the time to talk and being honest with him. He promised me he would try to give life his all, even when things got tough.

The following week, the coach saw that same student during practice and noticed a change. He was more focused, more dedicated, and more motivated than before. He was taking on challenges and responsibilities and giving his all during practice. Afterward, the student told the coach he had found a renewed purpose and was excited to see where his dedication would take him. The coach was proud of him and knew he had taken the first step toward achieving his goals. The student learned more challenges would be ahead but was confident that he had the strength and determination to overcome them.

Life is difficult, but giving up is not the answer. Students must know the importance of dedication and commitment. Everyone has the potential to achieve all their goals, but it takes hard work and perseverance. Be proud on your journey; support will always be there to encourage, even when things get tough.

Octopus Story

I devised a scenario to tell my son about the importance of focusing on his personal goals. An octopus has nine brains; the central brain resembles your main world. All your goals, dreams, and ambitions are in the center. And the tentacles represent everything going on around you. One could be for a friend, homework, internet time, gaming time, playing outside, time on the phone, wasting time, and chores. When you leave your central hub to adventure down one of the tentacles, all these obstacles will take your time away.

If you spend too much time on a tentacle, it will start swinging around, consuming your energy and preventing you from doing what you need to focus on. Limit the time on each tentacle, knock out what you must, but be practical so you can return and work on your priorities in life. Otherwise, the world takes advantage of you; people will step on you to get where they're going. Chores are fundamental; as you grow older, duties increase tenfold, and you don't want things to pile up and swarm you with urgency, causing stress and feeling overwhelmed. Some of the reasons your parents have you make your bed are for two reasons. First, you're working by cleaning up after yourself; second, you've accomplished something first thing in the morning. As you get older, you'll receive more chores, dishes, laundry, lawn, vacuuming the house, and your homework.

If you reach adulthood and cannot take care of yourself, it'll be quite a problem. When the day comes that you're in an apartment or a house, you'll need to cook, clean counters, feed the animals, and pay the bills while maintaining the property. Failure to complete your chores promptly will cause anxiety as you'll become overwhelmed by everything around you. That's why it's so important to finish everything once it's needed to be accomplished to prevent life from piling up.

Opinions are like Buttholes

My Grandpa Ron always said that opinions are like buttholes. Everyone has one, but that doesn't mean they're worth listening to. As a teenager, it's easy to get caught up in what other people think of us. We worry about fitting in, being famous, and pleasing others. But the truth is, other people's opinions don't matter as much as we think they do. It's important to remember that people can be mean and ugly. They may criticize, judge, or try to bring us down. But their negativity says more about them than it does about us. We shouldn't let their opinions define us or dictate how we live our lives.

Instead, we should focus on our thoughts and feelings. What do we believe in? What are our values and priorities? What makes us happy and fulfilled? These are the questions that matter most. Of course, it's easier said than done. Ignoring negative opinions and criticism is hard, especially from people we care about. But by building our confidence and self-esteem, nobody can get in our way once we learn to trust our instincts.

Accomplish setting your goals and working towards them one step at a time; you want to see yourself getting one step closer. When we have a clear sense of purpose and direction, it's easier to tune out other people's opinions and focus on what matters to us. Whether getting good grades, pursuing a hobby, or making new friends, having a goal can give us a sense of accomplishment and purpose. Another way to build confidence is by surrounding ourselves with positive influences. If you're trying to get better grades, hang around the A+ students, get involved, and be proactive. People love to help each other, and teens love guiding one another as they feel more influential. Ask your teachers for additional guidance and advice in your troubled areas. Don't allow your environment to reflect adverse outcomes because you didn't speak up.

When surrounded by people who believe in us, believing in ourselves is more effortless. Of course, remember that we don't have to please everyone. We can't control other people's opinions and shouldn't try to. If someone dislikes or disapproves of us, that's their problem, not ours. We should focus on being true to ourselves and living according to our values and beliefs. At the same time, being kind and respectful towards others is essential. We should avoid being judgmental or critical of others, even if we disagree. After all, we wouldn't want someone else to judge us based on their opinions and biases.

Grandpa was right; opinions are like buttholes. They're everywhere, but not all of them are worth listening to. As teenagers, we should focus on our thoughts and feelings and not let other people's negativity bring us down. By building our confidence, surrounding ourselves with positive influences, and staying true to ourselves, we can overcome the negativity and achieve our goals. So, let's ignore the haters and focus on you being awesome. In the future, high school is over, college is over, and life is still there! Guess what? Developing awesomeness in your younger years continues in your adult years. Get your butt in gear; you need to live your life, not listen to any of your own excuses!

Embrace the journey that lies ahead. Each affirmation and positive thought is a step forward in your battle against anxiety and depression. With the power of affirmation, you are not just surviving but thriving. You are not just fighting; you're winning. Embrace your power, harness it, and see the incredible difference it can make in your life. You have all you need within you. Believe it. Affirm it. Live it.

After weaving through the twisting roads of this journey and exploring the highs and lows of anxiety and depression, I know you will do extraordinary things. This is not the end; it's a new beginning, a beacon of hope in an often-clouded world. You've heard stories, shared experiences, and gained insight into the monumental battles we've discussed. Now, it's time to reflect and inspire. Remember, anxiety and depression aren't signs of weakness; they are battling millions of people like you. Recognize that these feelings can be managed; with time and patience, you'll find a balance that works for you.

Let's revisit an example that many of us can relate to. Imagine you're learning to ride a bike. At first, you're bound to stumble and fall. The first few rides may be filled with fear, uncertainty, or pain. But what do you do? Do you give up? No. You get back on the bike. Each time you fall, you rise again, a bit wiser and more decisive. You keep going because mastering these skills will open up a world of possibilities—adventures, freedom, and joy. Similarly, your journey with anxiety and depression can feel like learning to ride that bike. It's going to be tough. There may be days when it feels like the whole world is spinning. But remember, each stumble and fall is part of the journey. Each time you get back up, you are one step closer to understanding yourself.

Think about how far you've come; picture the resilience you've shown, the patience you've practiced, the understanding you've gained. Use these tools to move forward. Write your own story at your own pace. It's not a race; it's your journey and yours alone. Remember, the goal isn't perfection; it's progress. Don't forget that there are people who want to help you. Friends, family, teachers, and counselors are all part of your support network. Let them in and share your thoughts and feelings because no one is meant to fight this battle alone.

Just like you wouldn't expect to master the bike on the first try, don't expect to conquer anxiety and depression overnight. It's a process, one that requires patience and understanding. It's okay to have bad days. It's okay to feel down sometimes. What's important is that you keep trying, keep pushing forward, and keep believing in yourself.

When life gets dark and complex, it may seem impossible to find happiness. Remember that there's always a light at the end of the tunnel. You can find joy even in the darkest times by flipping the switch and shedding light on your path. Don't let the fear of the unknown keep you from taking that first step. Instead, trust that things will improve and remember that it's always darkest just before dawn.

Each day is a fresh opportunity, a new canvas to paint a picture of your life. You can write your own story. It can be characterized by resilience, courage, growth, and a journey towards understanding and healing. Victory is always within reach for those who refuse to give up the fight. With a steadfast commitment to never give up, success is always possible. So, keep fighting, and don't let life's challenges bring you down. Remember that every step forward, no matter how small, brings you closer to the finish line.

As we close this book, the rest of your story remains to be written. Remember, you're stronger than you think, braver than you feel, and loved more than you know. Keep going, keep growing, and keep shining. The world needs your light. I really hope you enjoyed this book. Recommend it to others who could use some assistance. There's so much of this information that applies to adults as well as teens because an adult is a teenager with a few more years of experience.

It's just like martial arts.

A black belt was a white belt that didn't give up.

I hope you've enjoyed the book. Please leave a book review with your thoughts.

My website is available if you need to contact me with anything on your mind.

www.GarySPark.com

www.ingramcontent.com/pod-product-compliance
Lightning Source LLC
LaVergne TN
LVHW051054080426
835508LV00019B/1870